Home grown Tommy K's
picked by L i b i a n a . k

PREPPED!

Vanessa Kimbell

PREPPED!

'Gorgeous food without the slog – a multitasking
masterpiece for time-short foodies'

ENGLISHMUM.COM

Vanessa Kimbell

SPRING HILL

To my darling children, Libiana, William and Isobel, to the love of my life, Alastair, and to my wonderful mother, who taught me to cook. For all the wonderful meals we have shared and for all the laughter, picnics, teatimes, parties and food to come. Life is delicious.

Published by Spring Hill, an imprint of How To Books Ltd.
Spring Hill House, Spring Hill Road
Begbroke, Oxford OX5 1RX, United Kingdom
Tel: (0)1865 375794
Fax: (0)1865 379162
info@howtobooks.co.uk
www.howtobooks.co.uk

First published 2011

How To Books greatly reduce the carbon footprint of its books by sourcing its typesetting and printing in the UK.

British Library Cataloguing in Publication Data
A catalogue record of this book is available from the British Library.

ISBN: 978 1 905862 56 6

Produced for How To Books by Deer Park Productions, Tavistock, Devon
Designed and typeset by Ian Hughes, Mousemat Design Limited – www.mousematdesign.com
Edited by Jamie Ambrose
Photography by Brian Dunstone and Tony Hardacre
Printed and bound in Great Britain by Bell & Bain Ltd, Glasgow

Contents

Introduction

Fitting everything in is a balancing act for busy people. Multitasking is how many of us get the most out of our time. When I exercise, I socialise with friends. When I chat on the phone, I tidy up. When I make supper, I help the children with their homework. *Prepped!* is the way I multitask food. It's how I have it all, so to speak!

As a trained chef I love food – *really* love it. I'm a time-short foodie who wants to eat delicious lunches and scrumptious suppers. That's why I use every trick there is to make my time work for me, and it's these tricks you now have in your hands, within the covers of *Prepped!*

Each chapter focuses on a specific flavour, featuring straightforward recipes that use simple ingredients – but with a difference. On each page you'll find sophisticated linking and layering techniques that let you alter the flavours and moods of your dishes at the drop of a hat. Turn the page to see how it works. The food in this book isn't complicated, but it is complex in terms of its flavours and presentation.

The recipes and tips in *Prepped!* cover every aspect of real life, from the unexpected guest or the Friday-night-straight-from-work supper party to canapés and cocktails for those fabulous grown-up moments. And of course, I've included priceless picnic food for whenever you get a chance to grab that glorious afternoon in the park.

The truth is we do want it all: the romance of enjoying time and gorgeous food with friends and family, but without slogging away in the kitchen for hours on end. Life should be full of spur-of-the-moment picnics, supper parties, country walks, fun time, sunshine and laughter. Food and eating are integral to these treasured moments. Whether it's food gifts, divine cakes, teatime treats, simple dinner-party fare or fast food for instant hospitality, it's about being able to make it happen.

To take that space and time to enjoy life's opportunities, you have to be ready. Being spontaneous really means being prepared.

So don't just dream about it; multitask it, plan it, be in control and make every day special.

Be delicious. Be *Prepped!*

Vanessa X

How to use *Prepped!*

The word *prepped* is used in professional kitchens. It covers everything chefs do to plan and prepare before they start cooking and service begins.

Prepped! takes a similar approach to your home kitchen: it's all about what and how you're planning to cook. In practice, each concept is pretty obvious: make double and use the other half in another recipe; have base flavours you can swap at a moment's notice; make extra and freeze. There are links throughout the book to help you do this. Using *Prepped!* is really all about how you *choose* to use it and what you are planning to cook. One recipe leads naturally to another. It's a mix-and-match of techniques to help you be efficient, save time and effort, and get ahead. Rather than asking you to follow an instruction manual, just look at some examples:

• Mackerel & Dill Pâté (page 43): make double and the other half makes Mackerel & Rhubarb Pasta (same page) for supper. Result? A main course and a starter from the same ingredients, and one lot of washing up.

• Chocolate Truffle Ganache (page 212) makes truffles for a gift. But leave half the mix in the bowl, place it over a bain marie, and then make Chocolate, Cardamom & Orange Gelato (page 215). Two different recipes from the same ingredients, same shopping, and just one extra saucepan to wash!

• When making Caraway & Lemon Pumpkin Soup (page 184), half can be transformed in minutes to make the filling for Pumpkin Pie (page 187) by adding eggs and sugar. The prep for the pie is already done.

In much the same way, Elderflower & Rose Syrup (page 14) can be made almost instantly into Elderflower Sorbet (page 22) or a cocktail (page 17) for a dinner party. And the Spiced Orange & Clove Brandy (page 242) you make as a gift also features in the Festive Cocktail on the same page as well as in Instant Cranberry & Brandy Mincemeat (page 253). So you have a delicious get-ahead gift and the basis for a really outstanding fruity mincemeat and a cocktail!

When using *Prepped!* the most important thing to remember is to look at and use the KEY recipes in each chapter first. Whenever a key recipe appears in the ingredients for another recipe, the symbol > guides you to a 'Links' box on that page, which lists exactly where you'll find it.

Flavoured sugars and syrups are the key recipes that link the most with other recipes. These are:

- Elderflower & Rose Syrup
- Rhubarb Syrup
- Lavender & Lemon Syrup
- Lemon Syrup
- Lavender Sugar
- Vanilla Sugar
- Cardamom Sugar
- Orange & Clove Sugar

As well as the 'Links' boxes, you'll find 'Tips & Uses' listed for most recipes, with suggestions on other ways of using and serving the recipes, as well as hints on the most time-efficient ways to make them. Note: the prep times listed are judged from the moment the ingredients are all lined up, ready to use – just like they would be for those professional chefs I mentioned earlier.

I'm often asked about special equipment, but the only thing I use a lot is my KitchenAid mixer. I find it invaluable, but any good mixer will be fine. My pan sizes may sometimes be larger because I often make double a recipe to freeze, but this shouldn't affect your use of any recipes here.

Many of the recipes in *Prepped!* call for fresh, seasonal ingredients, but if you're buying this book out of season, don't despair! Be resourceful and look for really good-quality replacements. It's what I'd do if I wanted to make something using elderflowers in December! There are lots of commercial syrups on supermarket and deli shelves, and plenty of homemade jams at farmers' markets, but take a moment and put a reminder in your diary to make your own in the appropriate month.

My final bit of advice on how to use this book? Take *Prepped!* to bed with you! Get an idea of how it works *before* you start cooking – but don't be surprised if you find yourself back downstairs in the kitchen, prepping one of the sugars in your dressing gown!

Publisher's Foreword

Vanessa arrived at Spring Hill with a basket full of Vanilla and Rhubarb Cupcakes (page 33) on a sunny day in June. We met outside because she had decided that the best way to explain the concept for *Prepped!* was to lay it out as a flow chart on card.

Our patio became a sea of paper showing us how she planned to link recipes within each 'flavour chapter', and how different recipes could be mixed and matched using different flavours. In spite of the usual Spring Hill breeze doing its best to rearrange the mass of paper – and our two dogs wanting to join Vanessa in her demonstration – we soon saw her concept unfold and had no hesitation in deciding there and then that we wanted to publish *Prepped!* As Giles and I ate the cupcakes, we also realised that Vanessa is an amazing cook, blending flavours effortlessly. I can honestly say that they were the best cupcakes I had ever tasted!

We've never been slow at Spring Hill in wanting to get on with exciting new concepts when we see them, so Vanessa was suddenly under huge pressure to get the book written and the photographs taken in order for us to follow the seasonality of the flavours. She has years of experience of getting super food on the table with minimum fuss, and she has put this knowledge into the recipes contained in *Prepped!* We very much hope you enjoy the result.

We're constantly having family and authors dropping in at Spring Hill, so the book will be very well used here. Personally, I'm looking forward to having a cupboard full of flavoured sugars, and jams and syrups, so that – like Vanessa – I, too, can produce fantastic food, bursting with flavour, at the drop of a hat.

Nikki Read
Spring Hill

Elderflower

*Frilly, frothy heads
of white elderflowers
may be seen from June
to mid-July in most
hedgerows throughout
Britain. Their
sweet-smelling flowers
are easy to find;
nevertheless, do avoid
gathering polluted ones
at the edge of busy roads.*

*Elderflower & Rose
Syrup is the basis for
all recipes in this
chapter, lending its
flavours to both sweet
and savoury dishes
as well as to a saucy
cocktail. Elderflower
cordial can be bought,
but a superior syrup
can be made much more
economically at home.
It's so straightforward:
just stir, leave
and strain.*

Elderflower & Rose Syrup

This pink, floral, slightly tart yet sweet liquid makes a superb gift. Yes, you can buy it, and if you're reading this in the other ten months of the year when it's out of season, then by all means do. But promise yourself you'll make the effort to create your own. A pretty bottle brought to a dinner party makes a gift that will be remembered. This is a versatile little number that will take you places.

Makes 1.5 litres
Prep time 25 minutes
(plus 24 hours to steep)
Cooking time 20–30 minutes
Suitable for freezing Steep the flowers in hot water for 24 hours and freeze, then defrost and add the other ingredients.

30 pure-white elderflower heads
8 heads red/pink scented roses
2kg caster sugar
1 litre water
Rind and juice of 2 lemons
75g citric acid

1 Give the flowers a good shake to ensure there are no insects hiding among the petals. Trim any stems and leaves. Remove the petals from the roses and discard the stems.

2 In a large pan, heat the sugar and water, stirring until all the sugar has dissolved. Allow this to cool, and when the water is 'hand hot', add the flowers and rose petals, lemon rind and juice and citric acid. Stir well, cover and leave for 24 hours, stirring occasionally.

3 Strain the syrup either through muslin or an old clean cotton tea towel placed in a colander, ensuring none of the bits get through. Decant into sterilised bottles and seal.

4 Keep in the fridge for up to 6 weeks.

LINKS

> Elderflower & Rose Syrup is linked to all recipes in this chapter.

Also use it instead of Rhubarb Syrup or Lemon Syrup in the following:
> Mackerel & Rhubarb Pasta/Mackerel & Dill Pâté, page 43
> Rhubarb & Custard Ice Cream, page 51
> Lemon & Chilli Oysters, page 86
> Hot or Cold Lemon Chicken Rice Salad, page 98

TIPS & USES

● Use only pure-white elderflowers. Brown ones will taint the flavour.

● Citric acid should be available from a local chemist, from brewing and winemaking shops or online. In this recipe it does two things. Firstly, it acts as a natural preservative, and secondly its sourness counteracts sweetness, which in turn allows the elderflower – not the sugar – to be the first thing you taste.

● This syrup makes a perfect topping for vanilla ice cream, and I love to drizzle mine into plain buttered couscous. I also use this to drizzle over Lemon Cake (page 105). Delicious!

Ginger von Tease

If one thing says 'party' to me, it's a cocktail. It's a promise. It's 1950s glam. In homage to burlesque dancers, my sister, Fleur, and I decided this cocktail should be called Ginger von Tease. The other reason I love this drink is that non-alcoholic cocktails seem to centre on fruit juice, especially orange. One can only drink so much fruit juice in an evening, and Ginger von Tease without the gin makes a much more interesting alternative for those who've drawn the short straw of designated driver. Chin chin!

Makes 1

1 part Elderflower & Rose Syrup **>**
1 part gin
2–3 parts ginger beer
A cocktail cherry, to garnish

TIPS & USES
● This also works well with Champagne instead of ginger beer, but be warned: you may actually think you *are* a burlesque dancer after drinking it!

1 Pour the syrup into a cocktail glass, followed by an equal measure of gin.

2 Top up with 2–3 parts ginger beer. Stir gently and add a cocktail cherry to serve.

> **LINKS**
> > Elderflower & Rose Syrup, page 14
> > Try using Rhubarb Syrup (page 36) with bitter lemon and vodka, and Lemon Syrup (page 82) with gin and tonic.

Lime & Elderflower Salad Dressing

There is hardly a salad that I wouldn't put this dressing on: it has both zing and sweetness. Children seem to enjoy it, too. The quantities here make enough for two salad portions, give or take. You may only want a small amount, but I always find it just as easy to make up a full batch by measuring a third each of the lime, syrup and oil into a clean maple syrup bottle. Adjust the lime juice to suit your taste – but not too much! I don't add salt or pepper. You can if you want, but I think they're best used directly on the salad, post-dressing.

Serves 2
Prep time 5 minutes

1 large lime (for zest and 3 tbsp juice)
3 tbsp Elderflower & Rose Syrup **>**
3 tbsp olive oil
½ tsp Dijon mustard (optional)

1 Using a zester, remove slivers of zest from the lime before cutting it in half to squeeze out the juice.

2 Put all the ingredients into a clean bottle or jam jar, adding the zest last; this ensures it doesn't end up stuck to the bottom of the bottle. Do check that the lid is on properly or you will end up with a comedy moment! Shake to mix.

3 This will keep happily in the fridge for 1 week. However, remember to bring it out a good half-hour before serving to warm up to room temperature, and give it a good shake before using.

TIPS & USES

● This dressing works on many other salads, and it goes particularly well with oily fish. Drizzle it over couscous with watercress and hot smoked salmon. Its sweetness works really well with peppery rocket.

● It also works beautifully on sliced tomatoes and mozzarella, Italian-style.

● If you're taking a salad to a party or a barbecue, a bottle of this dressing makes a rather fine gift.

LINKS

> Elderflower & Rose Syrup, page 14
> For a zesty alternative, swap the Elderflower & Rose Syrup for Lemon Syrup on page 82.
> Use the same principle with the Rhubarb Syrup (page 36) to go over baked chicory.
> For a terrific combination of flavours, serve with Pork Knuckle Terrine (page 94).
> Hot or Cold Lemon Chicken Rice Salad, page 98
> Plum, Mint & Couscous Salad, page 164
> Makes a good companion for the Caraway Sticky Rice Balls on page 192.

Pear, Walnut & Beetroot Salad

This salad has a French feel. The cooked-beetroot softness balances the juicy pears, while the added sweetness of elderflower is tempered by tart lime. Tossing the pears in lime juice also prevents the oxidisation process that makes fruit go brown, so you can have this ready about half an hour before your guests arrive. Scale it up to lunchtime fare by adding a scattering of feta and serving it with French bread to soak up the dressing.

Serves 2
Prep time 5 minutes

A good handful of green, crunchy
  salad leaves
1 pear
Juice of 1 lime
2 cooked (but not pickled) beetroot
12 walnut halves
Lime & Elderflower Salad Dressing **>**

1 Arrange the green salad leaves on plates or bowls.

2 Slice the pear and toss it in the lime juice. Slice the beetroot into circles and arrange neatly. Beet juice has a tendency to dribble over the plate, so for an arty-looking salad it's worth keeping a piece of kitchen roll under the beets until they're in place.

3 Arrange the walnuts on the salads. Should you have any elderflowers in season, scatter a few of the edible blossom heads around.

4 Dress the salad just before serving. If you dress it too early, the lettuce will go limp and lose that crispy, fresh look. I often put the dressing in a small jug and leave it to my guests to dress their own salads according to taste.

TIPS & USES
● Works well as a starter for a late summer supper.

● A super picnic salad, and delicious with added slices of orange.

LINKS
> Lime & Elderflower Salad Dressing, page 18
> Use it as a natural partner for Lavender Salmon (page 68), or Pork Knuckle Terrine (page 94).
> For a light lunch, add a soft, crumbly goats cheese with slices of Caraway Soda Bread, page 196.

Elderflower Sorbet

Unlike today's formal interval, nineteenth-century Italian opera had no break. Instead, there was an aria di sorbetto, *or 'sorbet aria', which allowed the audience to chat and buy sorbet from vendors towards the end of the second act. The idea of being able to chat and wander about during an opera, almost participating in the performance, really appeals to me. Sorbet has lost its fun and become prim and proper, offered as a low-fat option for dieters (where's the fun in that?). This, coupled with the move from formal dinner party to informal supper has meant that we miss out on sorbet. Bring back the informality! Whack* La Traviata Brindisi *(Verdi) on the stereo, serve this as a pre-mains treat and I guarantee an Italian moment.*

Makes 4
Prep time 3 minutes
Setting time 2 hours
Suitable for freezing

300ml Elderflower & Rose Syrup >
300ml bitter lemon
300ml water

1 Mix the Elderflower & Rose Syrup, bitter lemon and water together and pour into an ice-cream maker. Follow the manufacturer's instructions.

2 If you haven't got an ice-cream maker, it's not a problem. What the ice-cream maker does is move the liquid while it's freezing to stop crunchy ice crystals forming, which would otherwise ruin the texture. It's nothing a timer and electric mixer can't do instead. Pour the liquid into a wide, shallow bowl (such as a lasagne dish) and freeze for 1 hour. Remove from the freezer and beat. Return to the freezer. Repeat the process 2 more times. I set the timer on my mobile to repeat every hour, more often than not because I've left the kitchen and forgotten about the sorbet after the first stir!

TIPS & USES
● Mixing the liquid as it freezes breaks down the size of the ice crystals to give you a smooth ice, so ensure if you're making this by hand to mix it at least 3 times.

● If you have any leftover Champagne, use it instead of the bitter lemon. However, you'll also need to reduce the water by 150ml.

● On occasion if there's no ice in the house I use this sorbet as a base for a cocktail. Scoop a dollop into a cocktail glass, add a tot of vodka, a dash of tonic and mix.

LINKS
> Elderflower & Rose Syrup, page 14.
> To make Rhubarb Sorbet, use the Rhubarb Syrup on page 36 instead of Elderflower & Rose.
> Use the Lemon Syrup on page 82 instead of Elderflower & Rose to make a Lemon Sorbet.

Baked Trout with Chilli & Elderflower

A superb emergency lunch. I use trout fillets from the freezer: it's so fast and seriously simple. This dish came about as I was trying to recreate a meal I had in Hoi An, Vietnam, when I discovered a cookery school by the side of a river. I booked onto the course and, early the following morning, went upriver in a fishing boat operated by a toothless fisherman to catch the ingredients we needed. We returned to the school and cooked it there and then: fish for breakfast served with sticky jasmine rice – magical. This recipe is as close as I can get to replicating that melange of sweet, sour and salty. The original dish had floral tones from local, highly aromatic herbs, but using my Elderflower & Rose Syrup reproduces the effect exceedingly well. I'm quite certain the fisherman, should he ever have the chance to try it, would acknowledge the similarity instantly.

Serves 2
Prep time 5 minutes
Cooking time 18–25 minutes
Suitable for freezing

2 whole trout, cleaned and gutted
20g unsalted butter
2 chillies
4 stems of fresh basil
A pinch of salt
3 tbsp Elderflower & Rose Syrup **>**
Juice of 1 lime
2 fresh dill stalks, to serve

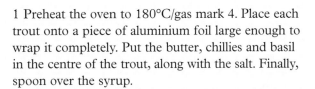

1 Preheat the oven to 180°C/gas mark 4. Place each trout onto a piece of aluminium foil large enough to wrap it completely. Put the butter, chillies and basil in the centre of the trout, along with the salt. Finally, spoon over the syrup.

2 Wrap up the trout as though you're making a tent. It needs to be sealed, but leave plenty of air at the top for the fish to steam in.

3 Bake for about 18–25 minutes. Cooking times vary, so check the recommended baking time against the weight of your trout.

4 Remove the basil and chilli before serving. Squeeze over the lime juice and sprinkle with dill.

LINKS
> Elderflower & Rose Syrup, page 14
> Serve with Pear, Walnut & Beetroot Salad, page 21.
> This recipe also works with Rhubarb Syrup (page 36) or Lemon Syrup (page 82).

TIPS & USES
● This dish works with other oily fish, including salmon, tuna and mackerel. It makes a simple supper-party dish as it's so quick to prepare, and is perfect for unexpected guests. Keep a pack of frozen fish on hand so you can cook it straight from the freezer.

● Great for a picnic – I cook the fish as fillets and leave the foil on until it's time to eat.

● A super barbecue addition, especially as you can prep it a good few hours before it needs to be cooked.

Baked Peaches in Elderflower & Rose Syrup

Sweet, juicy firm peaches topped with an almond filling, drizzled with Elderflower & Rose Syrup and served with a dollop of whipped cream… these are heavenly! Just make sure the peaches aren't overripe; otherwise they won't hold together. If I feel the need to impress, I serve these at a supper party, matching the floral tones with a sweet dessert wine such as Monbazillac.

Serves 4
Prep time 5 minutes
Cooking time 15 minutes

4 peaches
Elderflower & Rose Syrup **>** (to drizzle)

For the filling
80g ground almonds
40g caster sugar
40g butter
1 large egg

TIPS & USES

● This recipe can be made with other fruit. Nectarines work well, as do pears.

● These are great as a cold sweet to serve on a picnic.

● Serve with natural yogurt and a sprinkling of granola for a special breakfast treat.

LINKS
> Elderflower & Rose Syrup, page 14
> Add another dimension to the filling by using Lavender Sugar or Cardamom Sugar (pages 58 and 226).
> For a more homely, autumn sweet, put the peaches in a bowl, puddled in homemade Vanilla Custard (page 118), or try them with Vanilla Ice Cream, also on page 118.

1 Preheat the oven to 170°C/gas mark 3.

2 Put all the filling ingredients into a bowl and mix well. If your butter is soft, then you can mix this by hand; if not, chop the butter into cubes and whizz with a hand mixer.

3 Slice the peaches in half and remove the stones. Try to look for the natural shape in each peach: there's an easy split. If you have trouble removing the stone without squashing the peach, hold the peach in the palm of your hand and carefully tap the blade of a heavy knife on the stone. This should lodge the blade a small way into the stone; twist the knife and the stone will come out gently, still attached to the knife. Please pay attention: we're slicing peaches, not fingers, here!

4 Place the peach halves, hollow-side up, on a baking tray and spoon a dollop of the filling into each. Bake in the preheated oven for 12–15 minutes. If your peaches are soft, check them after 10 minutes. If they're firm, overcooking them will overbake the filling, so after 15 minutes turn the oven off and leave them in for another 10 minutes or so. The peaches carry on softening, but this won't ruin the filling.

5 Drizzle with 2–3 tablespoons of Elderflower & Rose Syrup and serve with plain whipped cream – not pouring cream. Putting pouring cream and the syrup together in a warm bowl will result in a curdled mess. Yet, strangely, if you add syrup while whipping the cream, as I do in several other recipes, then it doesn't curdle.

Elderflower & Champagne Jelly

I find it amusing to eat jelly. I'm four again! This is one of those dishes that looks exceedingly pretty and tastes as good as it looks – yet it still wobbles on your spoon! Jellies can make an appearance almost anywhere and be welcome. This recipe is inexpensive to make if you're using up the remains of a bottle: for instance, when half a bottle of bubbly is left over after a party. A word of warning, though: cheap fizz will sour jelly, so taste it before using – you may need to add a teaspoon or two of caster sugar and stir it in well. If you don't have Champagne, or want to make this recipe for children, ginger beer works really well, adding a good fiery kick, while bitter lemon will give your jelly a good sour base, too.

Serves 4
Prep time 5 minutes

150–200g mixed berries
300ml Elderflower & Rose Syrup **>**
250ml water
Gelatine granules (refer to packet
  for quantity)
300ml Champagne or similar bubbly

1 Scatter the fruit into whatever 1–1.2 litre dish or 4 small dishes you're going to use for serving your jelly.

2 Warm the Elderflower & Rose Syrup and water in a saucepan. When hot, sprinkle the gelatine granules onto the liquid. Whisk until dissolved. Remember to add the gelatine to the water, not the other way around; otherwise, the gelatine will end up as a mess of undissolved gloop at the bottom of the pan.

3 Once the gelatine has dissolved, add the Champagne. It's worth tasting at this point, and if you think the mixture is too sour, then add a teaspoon of caster sugar. It will taste quite strong, but this is fine; once it has set, the texture changes and calms the flavour's intensity.

4 Pour the liquid over the fruit and transfer the dish (or dishes) to the fridge to set.

TIPS & USES
● If preparing the jelly in advance, cover it with cling film to protect it from fridge odours.

● For vegetarians, you can use Japanese agar flakes, but the consistency will be nowhere near as firm and the jelly will be opaque.

● Only presentation dictates how you serve this dessert, so for a picnic use plastic cups, for a dinner party use tall, elegant cut-glass, and for a tea party use old-fashioned teacups and saucers. Enjoy!

LINKS
> Elderflower & Rose Syrup, page 14
> Rhubarb & Ginger Jelly uses
  300ml of Rhubarb Syrup (page 36)
  with 500ml of ginger beer: an
  unbeatable combination.
> Use Lemon Syrup (page 82) to
  make your jelly – it's lip-puckering!

Elderflower & Lime Macaroons

These delectable teatime treats are easier to make than their reputation suggests. The French use icing sugar and finely ground almonds for a smooth, high-colour look. These have more texture and are slightly more rustic. Nevertheless, the chewy, lime-green macaroon filled with light-pink elderflower cream is a very pretty combination and has perfect balance. Not too sweet, with lots of chewiness and a slight sour touch from the cherry jam, they are a real treat with a summer-afternoon cup of tea – and they also make super gifts.

Makes 20
Prep time 10 minutes for the macaroons,
15 minutes for decoration
Cooking time 30 minutes for resting,
plus 12–15 minutes to bake

For the macaroons
8 egg whites
350g caster sugar
12–15 drops green food colouring
200g ground almonds
Zest of 2 limes

For the filling
280ml double cream
80g icing sugar
4 tbsp Elderflower & Rose Syrup **>**
170g cherry or Rhubarb Jam **>**

To make the template
1 pencil
2 sheets of baking parchment
1 egg cup

TIPS & USES
● Use the leftover egg yolks to make
Cardamom & Basil Ice Cream,
page 234, or Rhubarb & Custard
Ice Cream, page 51.

● These will keep happily in an airtight
container for about a week.

1 Preheat the oven to 160°C/gas mark 3.

2 Whisk the egg whites until they form soft peaks.
Don't rush this bit – it will take about 10 minutes.
The macaroons will flop if you skimp on getting air
into your eggs before adding sugar.

3 Gradually add in the sugar until the mix is glossy
and thick. About halfway through add food
colouring: more drops if you like a deeper colour,
fewer for pastels. Using a large metal spoon,
sprinkle in the almonds and lime zest. Use a cutting
motion and fold the mixture back on itself. This
keeps the air in for light, fluffy macaroons. Don't
overmix; they need the air in them in order to rise.

4 Make a template for piping. Use a pencil to trace
egg-cup-size circles on the baking parchment; draw
lots of circles, then turn the paper over when you're
ready to pipe. Use a 1cm plain nozzle, fill a piping
bag two-thirds full and pipe small, biscuit-size
macaroons onto two baking sheets lined with the
circle-covered baking parchment.

5 Leave the macaroons for about 30 minutes before
baking – this improves the base. Bake in the oven
for about 12–15 minutes. Leave to cool before
removing from the parchment.

6 About 20 minutes before serving, beat the cream
and icing sugar together, adding the syrup at the
very end of whipping. Splodge the cream and jam
between the macaroons and serve.

LINKS

> Elderflower & Rose Syrup, page 14
> Rhubarb Jam, page 40
> Instead of Elderflower & Rose, use Rhubarb Syrup (page 36), to make Vanilla & Rhubarb Macaroons, or Lemon Syrup (page 82) to make Lavender & Lemon Macaroons.
> Try Lavender, Vanilla or Cardamom Sugar (pages 58, 108, 226) instead of plain sugar to alter the flavour.
> Instead of cherry or Rhubarb Jam, use Plum Jam (page 160) and Cardamom Sugar (page 226) to make Plum & Cardamom Macaroons.

Vanilla & Rhubarb Cupcakes with Elderflower & Rose Buttercream

I always think some of the best recipes come from slightly mad moments in the kitchen. Certainly, in the case of this delicious creation, I decided to add Elderflower & Rose Syrup to the butter icing simply because it was sitting next to the food mixer at the time. The Rhubarb Jam is the innovative part. It provides a sharp, sweet contrast to the butter icing while echoing the tartness of the syrup. The rose combines and lifts the vanilla. The result: a third dimension, the taste of a sunny day: perfect for teatime. These also make superb wedding cakes if you pile them high and decorate with geranium buds.

Makes 24
Prep time 15 minutes
Cooking time 25 minutes
Suitable for freezing Prior
to decorating

For the cupcakes
250g margarine, suitable for baking
250g Vanilla Sugar **>**
250g self-raising flour
4 large eggs

For the filling
300g icing sugar
250g butter
7 tbsp Elderflower & Rose Syrup **>**
1 drop red food colouring
170g Rhubarb Jam **>**

> **LINKS**
> **>** Elderflower & Rose Syrup, page 14
> **>** Rhubarb Jam, page 40
> **>** Make double the recipe and put half into a cake tin (it freezes) and use it to prep the base for Tipover Trifle (page 52). It's also the same recipe sponge used for the Victoria Sandwich Cake on page 176.
> **>** Vanilla Sugar, page 108

1 Preheat the oven to 180°C/gas mark 4.

2 Cream together the margarine and sugar and beat well until white and fluffy. Add 3–4 tablespoons of flour, mix well, then beat in the eggs – this prevents the mixture from curdling. Fold in the remaining flour. If the egg mixture has curdled, just keep adding the flour a little at a time, beating the mixture to ensure it is evenly distributed.

3 Line two 12-hole tartlet or muffin tins with cupcake papers, and fill each about two-thirds full with the mixture; this leaves room for rising. Bake in the oven for 20–25 minutes until firm to the touch. Cool on a wire rack.

4 Put the icing sugar and butter in a bowl. Beat this until it is light and fluffy, adding the Elderflower & Rose Syrup a tablespoon at a time.

5 If the mixture is too warm to pipe, transfer it to the fridge and leave until it has solidified enough. If for any reason it's too runny, just keep adding icing sugar, a tablespoon at a time, until you're happy with the result.

6 Scoop out a small walnut-size piece from the centre of each cooled cupcake. Spoon a teaspoon of rhubarb jam into the centre and replace the cut-out piece. Pipe the butter icing over and decorate.

Rhubarb

You have to flirt with Madame Rhubarb. Alone, she's sour. But add sugar and you still have to watch out: too little, and she's still sour; too much and you lose her acidic wit. I delight in finding the balance of that sour, cheek-sucking wince with the sugary fruit pleasure-hit from this exquisite spring treat. It's a principle that flows throughout this chapter: rhubarb's slender pink stalks are charming – but only when complemented.

Rhubarb tempers the richness of lamb, for example, and cuts through the sugariness of vanilla cake to accentuate the best qualities of the ingredients around it. I adore bringing the acidity out in slightly unexpected ways to add a burst of sharp sourness juxtaposed against sweetness. Its contrast and fruitiness not only make it fun to cook with but provide the things your taste buds love: stimulation, interest and contrast. Get rhubarb right and she'll be your true love for life.

Rhubarb Syrup

As a cordial this is just fabulous: this pink, intense syrup packs a really fruity punch. It's easy to make and is also a multipurpose staple – so have some ready in the fridge. If you're lucky enough to have a plant, then stash some young stems away in the freezer to make more in the winter.

Makes 700ml–1 litre
Prep time 10 minutes
Cooking time 45 minutes

Note The quantities here are made using very new, forced, fresh rhubarb. If your rhubarb isn't young and juicy, you won't get the yield of juice to make this amount of syrup – and the leftovers will be too tough to use in the other linked recipes.

1kg fresh or frozen rhubarb, chopped
180ml water
450g caster sugar

1 Put the rhubarb into a heavy-based saucepan. Add the water, cover and cook on a low heat until the rhubarb has liquefied. This can take up to 30 minutes, depending on the age and thickness of the stalks.

2 Strain off the liquid and pour it back into the saucepan. DO NOT throw away the leftover rhubarb. It makes the base for the filling for 2 Rhubarb Pies (page 48). You can divide it in half and freeze both batches until ready to bake the pies.

3 Return the pan to the heat and stir in the sugar.

4 Bring the mixture to the boil and boil for 2 minutes. Remove immediately from the heat and decant into a sterilised 1-litre jar or bottle, making sure it is well-sealed.

5 Keep for up to about 6–8 weeks in the fridge.

TIP
● This recipe works with plums; however, you'll need to add about 250ml of water to make plum syrup.

LINKS
> Use to make another version of the Ginger von Tease cocktail on page 17.
> Make Rhubarb Sorbet by swapping it for the Elderflower & Rose Syrup on page 22.
> Mackerel & Rhubarb Pasta/Pâté, page 43
> Use any leftover rhubarb, mixed with sugar to taste, for the Pavlova topping on page 44.
> Rhubarb & Custard Ice Cream, page 51
> Use either Vanilla Sugar (page 108) or Cardamom Sugar (page 226) for extra layers of flavour.

Spiced Lamb & Rhubarb Tagine

The prefect dinner-party dish. Rich lamb is undercut with sweet, sharp rhubarb and overlaid with eastern spices – it literally melts in the mouth. Working in the south of France, aged 18, I made friends with an exotic, raven-haired Algerian girl. I was invited to her house for supper. The air was thick with the smell of spices and steamed couscous. Her father smoked a heavy, sweet tobacco and spoke not a word to me after Bonjour, *but he watched every mouthful with fascination: it was as though I had dropped in from Mars. He studied me intensely for the entire meal. As you can imagine, I wanted to run a mile, but nothing was going to put me off eating this divine-smelling, sweet-spiced lamb. The taste was imprinted on my memory. This is my version, still utterly delicious, sans stares!*

Serves 4
Prep time 15 minutes
Cooking time 2 hours
Suitable for freezing

4 tbsp rapeseed or olive oil
1 red onion, roughly chopped
1.5kg lamb fillet, diced
6 cloves
16 juniper berries
10 cardamom pods
2 whole star anise
1 tsp paprika
1 tsp sea salt
2 heaped tbsp sugar
3 x 400g tins chopped tomatoes
250g chopped rhubarb

Couscous and fresh coriander, to serve

LINK
> Use any leftover meat to make pasties, following the method on page 191.

1 Preheat the oven to 175°C/gas mark 4.

2 Heat the oil in a large heatproof casserole. Add the onion and sauté for a couple of minutes until soft. Add the lamb a little at a time; this way it browns rather than stews for a better flavour.

3 Once the lamb is browned, add the spices, salt and sugar. Stir well and add the tomatoes and chopped rhubarb. Depending on the time of year, your rhubarb may be more or less sweet and you may need to adjust the sugar to reflect this.

4 Transfer to the oven and cook for 2 hours. If you have the time, allow this to cool and eat it the following day – this way, the spices will continue to develop. Otherwise, allow the pot to stand for 15–20 minutes before serving; this improves the texture of the meat. I usually use the oil off the top to put in the couscous instead of butter.

5 Serve on a bed of couscous scattered with chopped coriander.

TIPS & USES
● Mix 50/50 with mashed potato to make a superb filling for pasties. Remove any large spices first.

● This also makes a super base for a lamb pie: simply put it into a deep ovenproof dish and cover with pastry.

● This recipe works beautifully with venison.

Rhubarb Jam

Sweet, sour and lusciously thick, rhubarb jam transforms numerous dishes. It's spring in a pot. What I love most about this jam is that it's so versatile. With floral overtones, a pink hue and natural tartness it's delicious served over baked scones with a cup of Earl Grey tea, sandwiched in the middle of a vanilla cake, or as the base for trifle. Rhubarb Jam has qualities no other jam can mimic. Spare jars make superb presents, yet despite my generous suggestion, I confess to a certain reluctance to give them away!

Makes 9 x 450g jars
Prep time 35 minutes
Cooking time 15 minutes

2kg rhubarb, chopped
2kg jam sugar
Juice of 2 fresh lemons

LINKS
> Vanilla & Rhubarb Cupcakes, page 33
> Rhubarb Pavlova, page 44
> Rhubarb Pie, page 48
> Tipover Trifle, page 52
> Victoria Sponge Cake, page 238

1 Preheat the oven to 160°C/gas mark 3 and pop the jars (but not the lids) into the oven.

2 Put a small saucer in the fridge to chill.

3 Put the chopped rhubarb in a large saucepan, cover and heat gently for about 10 minutes. You're almost looking to 'melt' it; heated rhubarb turns from solid chunks into a thick liquid. Stir gently occasionally and keep the pan covered.

4 Once the consistency is liquid, add the sugar and stir. When the sugar has dissolved, bring the jam to the boil for about 5–6 minutes on a good bubble. Take the jars out of the oven.

5 While the jam boils, use a metal spoon (gently!) to skim off any froth (like soapsuds) that appears on the top. This will improve the clarity of the jam. Take care not to remove too much jam, though.

6 The jam is ready when it coats the back of a metal spoon. To test for setting point, take the pot off the heat and drop a teaspoon of jam onto the cold saucer from the fridge. Wait about 1 minute, then run a spoon through the centre; if it's ready, it should wrinkle. If it doesn't wrinkle, return the pan to the boil and repeat this process about 3 minutes later. Note: don't over-boil jam. The setting point should take no longer than 20 minutes at most to achieve.

7 Add the lemon juice. Stir well, then ladle the jam into the jars using a jam funnel. After 1 minute, pop the lids on; the heat from the jam will ensure they are sterilised. Don't worry if a lid isn't done up tightly; you can tighten it later once the jars have cooled.

Rhubarb Jam

Perfect Partners: Mackerel & Rhubarb Pasta & Mackerel & Dill Pâté

This is a favourite of mine: two results for one effort – the perfect linked recipe! What I love about this combination is that it gets you prepped for free. It's just what you need after a busy day at work when guests are coming for supper in the evening. Rhubarb Syrup sweetens the fish, the lemon adds a sour note and the salt picks out the mackerel's flavour, all enveloped in a creamy base, with the dill adding a light, fragrant, herbal lift. The pasta is quick to get on the table as a main dish, and for no extra effort you can transfer some of the sauce mix across. Hey, presto! You have a superb starter: the mackerel pâté is ready to chill.

Makes • Pasta for 4 & pâté for 4
  • *Or* mackerel pasta for 8
  • *Or* mackerel pâté for 8
Prep time 5 minutes
Cooking time 15 minutes for the pasta

600g cooked mackerel fillets (If baking
  your own, 600g whole fish yields
  approximately 300g mackerel, once
  bones and skin are discarded)
6 tbsp Rhubarb Syrup >
Juice of 2 lemons
300g soft full-fat cheese
2 good pinches of sea salt
Freshly ground white pepper to taste
A handful finely chopped dill,
  plus extra for sprinkling
¼ tsp paprika

500g pasta
Olive oil
Freshly grated Parmesan, to serve

TIPS & USES

● The pâté makes a superb sandwich filler. With a handful of watercress and a squeeze of lemon in a crusty roll, you can have a delicious and easy packed lunch.

● Use smoked mackerel for a variation.

● Substitute trout or salmon for mackerel – or for an emergency fast supper, use a tin of well-drained tuna with an extra squeeze of lemon.

1 Place the mackerel fillets into a bowl and break them up with a fork. Regardless of whether you've bought the fillets prepacked or baked them yourself, check through them and remove any stray bones.

2 Add the syrup, lemon juice and soft cheese and mix well. Add the salt, pepper and dill and give it a final good stir.

3 To make both pasta and pâté for 4, remove half the mixture (about 350g) for the pâté, put it into a large cling-film-lined dish and place it in the fridge to set; the rest will make a good-sized pasta sauce portion to serve 4 people. If you want all of this recipe to be the pâté, turn it out into a serving dish and leave in the fridge for at least 4 hours to set before dusting with paprika and serving.

4 Cook your pasta according to the instructions on the packet.

5 Drain the pasta, then add a tablespoon of olive oil and stir. Add the mackerel sauce and stir well. Serve immediately with grated Parmesan and extra dill sprinkled over it.

LINKS
> Use either Elderflower & Rose or Lemon Syrup – pages 14 and 82 – instead of Rhubarb Syrup.

Rhubarb Pavlova & Rhubarb Fool

These recipes are so similar yet offer different perspectives on the same ingredients. I fall back on them as a base option time and again. I often intend to make pavlova, but let's face it: if it isn't up to standard (which happens, even to me), it gets turned into fool. The difference between the two bases is texture. The pavlova's meringue base has a soft chewiness to it due in part to the vinegar and cornflour, while the fool meringue (which uses neither) has a dry crunch. Both meringues store for at least two weeks, so you're prepared at the drop of a hat for pavlova, fruit fool or just plain fresh fruit tumbled over tender marshmallow meringue. Being prepped for a summer pudding at a minute's notice means having a meringue in the cupboard.

Rhubarb Pavlova

Serves 4–6
Prep time 15 minutes
Cooking time 1 hour 35 minutes

Meringue Base
6 egg whites
300g caster sugar
1 tbsp white-wine vinegar
  ★(only for pavlova base)
1 heaped tbsp cornflour
  ★(only for pavlova base)

Rhubarb Pavlova
Prep time 15 minutes

300ml double cream
3 tbsp icing sugar
1 pot Rhubarb Jam **>** (or 450g stewed
  rhubarb mixed with 50g caster sugar)

Rhubarb Fool Made with Meringue
Prep time 12 minutes

Extra ingredients: 1 punnet of either
strawberries, blueberries, raspberries,
or a mixture of fruit

1 Preheat the oven to 150°C/ gas mark 2.

2 Before you begin, ensure your utensils are spotless. Don't use a bowl (such as plastic) that may harbour any grease, and be sure all utensils are dry. Meringues are sensitive and don't get on with moisture or fat.

3 To make the meringue base, whisk the egg whites until fluffy: 3–4 minutes should do. Once they're fluffy, white and form soft peaks, don't stop beating; just slowly add the sugar, a tablespoon at a time, until it is all dissolved. Tipping it all in at once knocks the air out of the eggs, and if you stop beating, you knock the air out when you start again, so a flow of continuous beating gets the best results. If making the pavlova recipe, now's the time to add the vinegar and cornflower (NOT needed if you're making meringues for the fool, though!).

4 Use a pencil and large dinner plate to trace a circle on the back of some baking parchment, then turn it over. Dollop the mixture onto the circle on the paper, turn the oven down to 140°C/gas mark 1 and bake for 1 hour 35 minutes. Remove from the oven and allow to cool.

5 To assemble your pavlova, whip the cream and icing sugar until thick. Not too thick, though: you need to drape it gently over the meringue. Spoon the Rhubarb Jam (or stewed rhubarb) on top of the cream and serve. If you have any geranium petals or other edible flower petals, use these to decorate.

Rhubarb Fool Made with Meringue

TIPS & USES

● Instead of 1 large meringue, make 8 small ones. They make stunning food gifts. Dust them with cocoa powder and edible glitter as a festive statement for a supper party.

● For an extra flavour layer, infuse your cream overnight with a few lavender flowers or cardamom pods, lemon rind, or orange zest and cloves for a Christmassy flavour.

1 Follow the instructions for making the pavlova's meringue base; HOWEVER, omit the vinegar and cornflour and turn the oven off and leave the meringue in the oven to cool.

2 Break the meringue into chunks and put some of these in the bases of 4 large or 6 medium glasses. Then layer the whipped cream and Rhubarb Jam among the glasses, scattering fruit throughout the cream and meringue chunks.

TIPS FOR SUCCESSFUL MERINGUES

● Meringue really is one of the simplest things to make, but it is very important to avoid getting any yolk in the egg whites. Fat in the yolk will ruin a meringue before you've even begun. I can't emphasise this enough. Even a teeny, tiny drop of egg yolk can spoil a meringue. If you do accidentally drop in some egg yolk, then don't use your fingers to remove it; this also transfers fat into the whites. Instead, use half an eggshell to scoop it up. Wipe around a bowl with a slice of lemon, then dry with kitchen towel to remove any possible trace of grease.

● Always use fresh eggs but never eggs laid the same day (these sometimes won't rise for some reason). Fresher eggs hold the air better. Old eggs split and the yolks run. Even older eggs are stink-bombs and the smell of sulphur is revolting. Trust me: old eggs *can* get mixed up with new ones. Dropping a stink-bomb in and ruining all your eggs is something you only do once. Lesson learned.

● I recommend a three-bowl approach to breaking eggs. Break every egg and separate it over one bowl; if anything is wrong, then you haven't contaminated your other eggs. Transfer each white to a separate bowl containing only whites, and tip each yolk out of its shell into another bowl containing only yolks.

● If using a gas oven, keep a close eye on the meringue base at the end of the cooking time. Gas can be a harsher heat than electric, so take extra care!

LINKS
> Use leftover rhubarb from making Rhubarb Syrup (page 36) mixed with sugar as the topping.
> Rhubarb Jam, page 40
> Use the spare egg yolks in either Rhubarb Ice Cream or Vanilla Custard, page 51 and 118.
> Use flavoured sugars in the meringue, such as Lavender, Vanilla or Cardamom Sugar (page 58, 108 or 226).
> Use Vanilla Vinegar (page 109) in place of regular vinegar.

Rhubarb Pie

This recipe is a freebie. I had spare shortbread dough and leftover rhubarb from making Rhubarb Syrup and it seemed such a shame to waste the stewed fruit. I was also making Baked Peaches, which uses a very similar topping, so it was a no-brainer. The sweet shortbread crunches under a tart layer of rhubarb, while the frangipane pulls it all together with a soft almond sponge. It's seriously good, and if you combine the two recipes, you get ahead and use the same utensils to minimise your washing up. Now that's smart cooking!

Makes 1 pie, to serve 8
Prep time 30 minutes
Cooking time 35–40 minutes

For the base
350g Lavender Shortbread dough >
   from page 75

OR

125g butter
190g plain flour
50g sugar

For the filling
300g very well-drained rhubarb
50g caster sugar

For the frangipane
100g butter, chopped
100g caster sugar
100g ground almonds
Drop of almond essence
2 eggs
50g plain flour
30g flaked almonds

1 Preheat the oven to 160°C/gas mark 3. Use 350g dough from the Lavender Shortbread recipe or make a new base by rubbing the butter and flour together into a bowl to make 'breadcrumbs'. Add the sugar. Bring together with a small amount of water, added a little at a time to form a dough. Press the dough into the base of a 24cm tin and blind bake for 15–20 minutes.

2 Prepare the filling by mixing the rhubarb with the sugar.

3 Next, make the frangipane topping. It's not strictly the traditional way, but it works and it's quick. Simply put all the ingredients (apart from the flaked almonds) in a mixing bowl and use a mixer with a cake-making blade on a high speed for 3 minutes. The frangipane will keep uncooked in the fridge for up to 4 days.

4 To assemble the pie, spread the rhubarb on top of the shortbread. It must be well-drained! Pour the frangipane topping over the rhubarb, ensuring that it covers it fully. Sprinkle the flaked almonds on the top and place on the middle oven shelf.

5 Increase the oven temperature to 180°C/gas mark 4. Bake for 35–40 minutes, or until the topping has risen, is firm to touch and is a beautiful golden brown.

LINKS
> The stewed rhubarb is left over from Rhubarb Syrup, page 36.
> Lavender Shortbread, page 75.

TIP
● Use different fruit for a different tart, but try to retain the tartness; gooseberries, blackberries or quinces are good choices. Just remember to drain the fruit well – otherwise the base will go soggy.

Double Cook: Vanilla Custard & Rhubarb & Custard Ice Cream

Done right, homemade vanilla custard is heavenly. Light, not too sweet and infused with vanilla to its deepest point, this custard makes any pudding shout with joy as you puddle it around a crumble or moist treacle sponge. What I just love about this recipe is that, for nothing more than a pour and scoop, I have a pot full of vanilla ice cream waiting, ready to be brought out at the right moment. It's a delight to have it prepped.

Serves 8–10
Prep time 10 minutes
Cooking time • Custard 20 minutes
              • Ice cream 4 x 5
              minutes whisking over
              3–4 hours

1 vanilla pod
1 litre full-fat milk
500ml double cream
10 egg yolks
200g Vanilla Sugar >
200ml Rhubarb Syrup >

LINKS

> Change this in an instant by using Elderflower & Rose Syrup (page 14) or Lemon Syrup (page 82) instead of Rhubarb Syrup.
> Rhubarb Syrup, page 36
> To make Lavender Ice Cream, use 175g Lavender Sugar (page 58) instead of Vanilla Sugar and infuse your milk for 4 hours with some lavender flowers – but leave out the syrup completely.
> Vanilla Sugar, page 108
> For a moreish Orange & Clove Ice Cream with warm, spiced undertones, use 175g Orange & Clove Sugar (page 245) instead of the syrup and infuse the milk with the zest of an orange overnight for a really orangey kick.

1 Put the vanilla pod, milk, cream, egg yolks and sugar in a heavy-based saucepan and stir over a low heat. Keep moving the liquid using a whisk.

2 Keep stirring as the custard thickens. This can take 15–20 minutes so take your time and don't be tempted to heat it quickly (you'll get scrambled eggs!). The mixture will thicken. When the custard coats the back of a spoon, remove it from the heat. It won't be thick like commercial custard; it's more like a very thick gravy in consistency. Remove the vanilla pod. Note: Don't throw your vanilla pod away. Rinse it well, dry it, and pop in your sugar jar to make Vanilla Sugar.

3 Take 750ml out to serve as Vanilla Custard, leaving the rest of the mixture in the saucepan to cool (you can also store this for up to 2 days in a clean, airtight container before making it into ice cream).

4 Transfer into an ice-cream maker and follow the instructions to make the ice cream. If you make this by hand, then you'll need to pour the mixture into a shallow freezer-proof container, freeze for about an hour and stir in the 200ml of Rhubarb Syrup. Whisk it every 35 minutes of so, 3–4 times as it is setting to prevent ice crystals forming and you will get a smooth result. (Use a timer to remind you: I often forget to go back and whisk!).

Tipover Trifle

This trifle is a cinch to assemble – perfect for a quick dinner-party pudding – and the leftover custard makes Vanilla Ice Cream. The name came from a dessert stand I put the trifle on. It looked fabulous, but as I served it all from one side it became unbalanced; before I knew it, the entire trifle had tipped over across my antique French lace tablecloth! I was red-faced, but my guests were undeterred and ate it anyway. The name just stuck. Another time, as a result of rushing this recipe one evening, the cupcakes came straight out of the oven and the trifle was put together while they were still hot. The custard was still hot, too, and my husband was in a terrible hurry to sample it. He declared it the nicest thing he'd ever eaten – hence the hot trifle recipe made it into Prepped! *It is absolutely delicious. With a large dollop of Rhubarb Jam underneath, a trifle has attitude, cutting through the cream and custard in a charming, yet tart, bite – hot or cold.*

Serves 8
Prep time 10 minutes

4 Vanilla Cupcakes > roughly broken
   into quarters, or 220g Madeira cake
5-6 tbsp Plum Brandy >
200g or ¾ pot Rhubarb Jam >
300ml double cream
A handful of edible flower petals

For hot trifle
Add 200ml hot Vanilla Custard >
   (or use bought) to the
   above ingredients

TIP
● Instead of assembling the trifle in one large dish, try dividing it into eight individual glasses, such as the one shown opposite, for an especially elegant touch.

To make cold trifle
1 Place the cupcakes at the bottom of a lipped pedestal dish. Make sure they are broken up into manageable chunks. Spoon over the brandy and muss up the sponge a little.

2 Spoon over the jam, then dollop on the whipped double cream evenly. Scatter edible flower petals on to serve.

To make hot trifle
1 Warm the cupcakes either in the oven for 5 minutes, or in the microwave for a few seconds. Put them in a heatproof dish, spoon the brandy over them, then spoon on the jam.

2 Pour over 200ml of piping hot custard and dollop on the whipped cream. Serve immediately.

> **LINKS**
> > Vanilla Cupcakes, page 33
> > Use Rhubarb or Plum Jam (pages 40 and 160).
> > Make the Vanilla Custard (page 118), take out the small amount you need for this recipe and make the rest into Vanilla Ice Cream.
> > Plum Brandy adds extra fruitiness (page 156).

100mph Rhubarb
& Cardamom Batter Cake

We all have those occasions when you suddenly find yourself needing to produce something out of thin air. Generally it's at the worst possible moment, when the very last thing you need to be doing is baking. I use this recipe, from my mum, as something to fall back on. If I forget I've invited someone for tea (which happens more often than I like to admit!) or I have an emergency pudding to produce, I can have it in the oven in under six minutes, with one bowl to wash up. It's a doddle!

Makes 12 small portions
Prep time 12 minutes
Cooking time 20 minutes
Suitable for freezing

230g self-raising flour
1 pinch of salt
50ml rapeseed oil
100g Cardamom Sugar **>**
220ml whole milk
1 egg
120g rhubarb, chopped

For the topping
4 tbsp Cardamom Sugar **>**
1 tbsp cinnamon or ginger powder
75g chopped walnuts

1 Preheat the oven to 175°C/gas mark 4.

2 Put the flour, salt, oil, sugar, milk and egg into a bowl and mix well.

3 Put the ingredients for the topping into a jam jar and shake well.

4 Pour the batter into a low, wide, greased baking tin. Spread it out evenly. Top with the chopped rhubarb.

5 Sprinkle the topping from the jar evenly over the top and bake in the oven for 18–20 minutes.

TIPS & USES
● Spoon the batter into 12 muffin cases for breakfast muffins.

● Makes a super packed lunch treat.

● Use pears or plums instead of rhubarb to make a cardamom and pear (or plum) batter cake.

LINKS
> Swap plain sugar for Vanilla Sugar (page 108) and use 3 small chopped cooking apples instead of rhubarb to make Vanilla & Apple Batter Cake.
> Serve it straight from the oven with Cardamom Custard (page 118) for pudding.
> Cardamom Sugar, page 226

Lavender in the kitchen

Varieties of lavender grown for perfume have vastly different properties to those of the cottage garden *Lavandula augustifolia* used for cooking. Perfume-lavender would be revolting in food, but it adds middle and top notes to a scent. And this is exactly how I would describe *L. augustifolia*'s use in cooking: it overlays a sweet, fruity, floral mintiness to food. It's really very hard to describe. Much easier to say trust me: try it.

You can cook with lavender in several ways, using the dried or fresh flowers, or lavender oil and essence. I cannot stress enough to use the right lavender. There are literally hundreds of varieties, but it's the bog-standard cottage garden species that gives the sweet vanilla tones and is perfect for culinary use. Hidcote, Munstead, Rosea... any *augustifolia* will be fine. If in doubt, check online and you'll see what it looks like. There are other species, and yes, you can use them, but be warned: they may be very strong and have a camphorous odour. Avoid these.

It is always worth checking food allergies with guests before you serve them any food, and lavender is no exception. To be fair, it is rare to have a reaction, but it's still worth asking.

Methods of use

The simplest way to impart lavender's flavour to food, which requires some patience, is to infuse it. Lavender-infused sugar, milk or cream creates a mellow, even flavour throughout a dish. If you use essence or oil, the strength of flavour can be overpowering, but fresh lavender is lighter and more floral than dried. You can use dried lavender, of course, but simply use half the amount you'd use for fresh. Dried herbs are always more concentrated than fresh ones, but do use the freshest dried herbs you can. Also check that your lavender isn't musty before you use it.

Gathering lavender

A final word of advice: when gathering lavender, the best flavour comes from unopened buds. Once opened, the flowers lose the essential oils that impart the flavour. Pick buds on a dry, sunny afternoon and dry your lavender upside down, spaced to allow air to move around the flowers, in a well-aired, dark environment. Two to three days is enough to dry lavender picked in this way, and by drying it in the dark, you keep the intensity of the colour. Store in an airtight container, out of sunlight. You should pick a fresh batch each year; if you don't have lavender in your own garden, visit one of the many pick-your-own farms – or you could be cheeky and ask a friendly neighbour!

Lavender

With its beautiful, full heads of blue, mauve, indigo and, yes, even pink, lavender is one of the most elegant and delectable tastes you can use in cooking. It is a kitchen chameleon. A relative of both mint and rosemary, this fragrant herb has the ability to meld the right tones into accompanying food, whether sweet or savoury. If lavender were a person, it would be someone who always manages to say the right thing at the right moment. It uses exactly the right tone to suit the dish it is in.

What is notable about cooking with lavender is that it works with both sweet and savoury, transforming the everyday into something remarkable just by turning up in the dish. Strawberries and cream become strawberries sprinkled with lavender sugar. Crème caramel becomes lavender-laced crème caramel. So thank goodness lavender is fashionable to cook with again. It was the height of sophistication in Elizabethan times, when it was said that Queen Elizabeth I would not sit at a table of food without a pot of lavender conserve to accompany it. Cooking with it fell out of fashion as the Puritans banned anything considered frivolous. I think there are far more interesting things to ban these days, so I believe lavender is here to stay.

Lavender Sugar

Flavoured sugar is one of the easiest ways I know of introducing new and exciting flavour layers into your desserts. And for a real taste of spring, lavender sugar is just the thing!

Makes 1kg
Prep time 5 minutes

1kg caster sugar
8 heaped tbsp dried culinary lavender

1 Combine the lavender and sugar in a 1.5-litre airtight jar. There should be space left at the top to allow the jar, when shaken, to disperse the lavender evenly.

2 Over the next 2 weeks give the jar a shake from time to time. Ideally, leave the sugar for 6 weeks for maximum strength, but even after 2 weeks there is usually enough flavour to cook with. You can top this jar up twice, then start a fresh one.

TIP
● If you're drying lavender from the garden, please make sure the buds are 100% dry before using.

LINKS
> Use instead of plain sugar in Baked Peaches in Elderflower & Rose Syrup (page 26), Rhubarb Pavlova & Fool (pages 44 and 47) and Chocolate Cookie Mix (page 206).
> See the following recipes in this chapter: Boozy Strawberries (page 72), Lavender Shortbread (page 75), Chocolate Cupcakes with Lavender Cream (page 76), Lavender & Lemon Cake (page 79).
> Lemon Cake, page 105
> Vanilla Custard, page 118
> Use instead of Vanilla Sugar in Rice Pudding (page 121), Crème Brûlée (page 122), and Vanilla Custard Ice Cream (page 118).
> Use instead of Cardamom Sugar to make Barfi, page 233.

Baked Goats Cheese
& Lavender Honey Toasts

This is a superb starter. It's light, delicious, sophisticated, yet quick and simple. It tastes fabulous and the combination of flavours works. There's a good crunch to the toast, the cheese oozes and is drizzled in sweet, aromatic lavender honey. Not bad at all when you think it's just posh cheese on toast!

Serves 4
Prep time 10 minutes
Cooking time 20 minutes

4–5 tbsp honey
3–4 fresh lavender heads (or 2–3 dried)
4 slices of rustic bread
160g goats cheese (Brie and Camembert
  also work well)
A handful of cress

1 Combine the honey and lavender in a saucepan and gently warm through until it is nearly boiling. Allow to cool and stand for a minimum of 4 hours, or ideally overnight. If it has set too hard, then warm it again to sieve out the lavender.

2 Preheat the oven to 160°C/gas mark 3.

3 Divide the goats cheese among 4 slices of crusty bread. Put on a baking tray in the oven for 15 minutes.

4 Remove from the oven. Drizzle with 1 tablespoon of honey, scatter the cress around the toast and throw some fresh lavender flowers over. Serve immediately.

TIPS & USES
● You can make a whole pot of lavender honey. For a 450g jar use about 8 lavender flower heads and follow step 1 before returning the honey to the jar.

● Lavender honey makes a delicious bedtime drink: add a tablespoon to a cup of hot milk and stir well.

● Lavender honey also makes an excellent addition to a salad dressing, using lime and a light olive oil in equal quantities. Shake well and drizzle over a salad.

● In all instances, dried lavender can be substituted for fresh, but you must halve the amount used, as the flavour of dried herbs is more intense than fresh.

LINKS
> Use Lavender Bread for the toast, page 71.
> Use the lavender honey on the Cardamom Honey Drizzle Fig Salad, page 230.

Lavender Lemonade

You can't beat old-fashioned lemonade. Well, actually you can, with Lavender Lemonade. If ever a match was made in heaven it's lavender and lemon. Combined, the two are like Ginger Rogers and Fred Astaire – and they will make your taste buds dance. In June, July and August you can make this using fresh lavender, but out of season use Lavender Sugar. Before diluting it into lemonade, what you have is a working syrup that can be used as a flavour base for cakes, salad dressing, buttercream and cocktails – so it's worth making extra.

Makes 1 litre
Prep time 25 minutes
Cooking time 5 minutes

20 lavender flowers (in bud)
500g caster sugar
500ml water
Zest and juice of 7 lemons

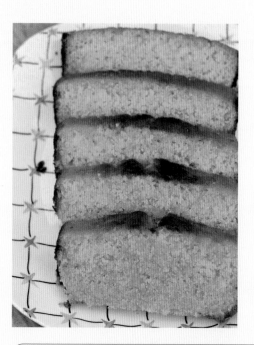

1 Put the lavender, sugar and water into a heavy-based saucepan and bring to the boil. Reduce the heat and simmer for about 5–6 minutes. Add the lemon juice.

2 Strain and allow to cool before transferring to a clean bottle. This should store in the fridge for 3–4 weeks. Dilute to taste for Lavender Lemonade, or use as Lavender & Lemon Syrup in the ways described below.

TIPS & USES

● To spruce up a shop-bought lemon cake, poke holes in the top with a skewer and drizzle with the syrup.

● There are times when I open a bottle of bubbly and it's too dry. Add this syrup to sweeten and lighten fizz and *ta dah!* You have a Lavender Champagne Cocktail.

● Mix one part syrup with one part light olive oil, a spoon of Dijon mustard and a squeeze of fresh lemon juice for a Lavender & Lemon Salad Dressing.

LINKS
> Lavender & Lemon Syrup also works well with fish. Using the Baked Trout with Chilli & Elderflower recipe (page 25) as a base, substitute this one for the Elderflower & Rose Syrup to create Lavender & Lemon Baked Trout.
> Lavender Sugar, page 58
> Use the syrup to drizzle over the Lavender & Lemon Cake, page 79.
> Use in place of Lemon Syrup in Lemon Cake, page 105.

Lavender Chicken

The sound of children playing and the smell of roast chicken are two things that say 'home' to me. The addition of lavender makes roast chicken smell so good that it's worth popping in and out of the house while it's cooking just to keep getting that initial hit. In the first instance the lavender adds an almost rosemary-like taste to the meat and a delicious summer sweetness to the gravy. I am roast-chicken-dependent, partly because I don't want to spend time over a hot stove in the summer, but also because the special addition of lavender turns an otherwise ordinary dish into something exceptional. People I've served this to always say how fabulous it is – and I then discover that they serve it to their own guests the following week!

Serves 6
Prep time 10 minutes
Cooking time 1 hour 30 minutes
Suitable for freezing

2 tsp good-quality sea salt
1 large chicken – about 1.6kg
12 sprigs of fresh lavender
Zest of 1 lemon, removed with
  a peeler (optional)
3 tbsp olive oil
Juice of 1 lemon
½ tsp sugar
2–3 tbsp cornflour
30ml single cream
Chives and lavender petals, to garnish

TIPS & USES
● Roast two chickens and you're prepped for anything, from spontaneous picnics to surprise supper guests. There are plenty of linked recipes you can make, or simply use spare chicken in sandwiches on Lavender Bread (page 71).

LINKS
> Use leftovers to make Chicken & Lemon Rice Soup, page 90.
> Use 400g cooked Lavender Chicken instead of ham hock in the risotto recipe on page 97.
> Use any leftovers to make Caraway Chicken Pasties, page 191.

1 Preheat the oven to 240°C/gas mark 9. Sprinkle salt over the top of the chicken and place 6 sprigs of lavender inside the cavity. If you want to make a Lavender & Lemon Roast Chicken, then now's the time to pop the lemon zest in the cavity, too.

2 Turn down the oven to 200°C/gas mark 6 and cook the chicken for 1 hour. Baste it with the juices and add 5–6 more sprigs of lavender to the juices in the bottom of the pan.

3 After 20 more minutes, check to see the chicken is cooked by inserting a skewer in the thigh; the juices should run clear. If they're still pink, return the bird to the oven for 10 more minutes and repeat the test.

4 Remove the chicken from the pan and set to one side to rest. These few minutes allow the meat to relax, which means it will be much more tender. In the meantime make the gravy. Strain the liquid into a gravy separator, returning the juice to the original baking pan. Put the pan over a medium heat and stir in the lemon juice and sugar. Always taste at this point and add more or less sugar, salt or water, depending on what you like.

5 To thicken the gravy, add a few drops of water to the cornflour to make it into a watery paste, then stir it into the gravy. Cook this through for a minute or so, still stirring.

6 Just before serving, stir 2–3 tablespoons of cream into the gravy. Slice the meat, cover with the lavender-infused gravy and use the remaining petals along with chopped chives to garnish.

Lavender Salmon

Because this dish can be served hot or cold, it makes easy, versatile eating. Served cold at a picnic with a lemon mayonnaise, it has an air of 1920s' decadence. It deserves a pretty checked blanket and chilled Chardonnay in real glasses. I love this as a dish to throw in the oven if you have an unexpected guest for lunch. They almost don't realise you've made it until you pull it out, ready and steaming, to serve with a lemony couscous. However you serve it, you'll find that lavender and salmon make a terrific duo. The oil in the fish seems to carry the flavour; it's delicate, aromatic and, I think, a romantic way of eating salmon.

Serves 4
Prep time 5 minutes
Cooking time 18 minutes

800g salmon fillet
1 tbsp butter
15 fresh sprigs of lavender
1 tsp honey
Salt

1 Preheat the oven to 175°C/gas mark 4.

2 Place the salmon skin-side down on a large piece of aluminium foil. Put the butter, lavender and honey on top, together with a sprinkling of salt – just a pinch will do. Pull up the sides of the foil to form a tent and squeeze the tops together so that there is space above the salmon for it to steam. This seems to give a better texture and improved taste to the fish.

3 Bake for 15–18 minutes. The time it takes to cook depends on the thickness of the fish, so check that the salmon is cooked by gently opening a strip of the flesh at the deepest point. It should all be a soft, cooked pink; if it is a darker, uncooked colour, return it to the oven for a few more minutes.

TIPS & USES
● If you're taking this on a picnic, leave it in the foil until ready to eat.

● I use this recipe on the barbecue and soak up the butter-infused juice with a fresh French stick.

● Fresh salmon is best, but there are plenty of choices in the supermarket for salmon that can be cooked straight from frozen, so keep some stashed in the freezer for unforeseen eating requirements!

● Salmon can be swapped for most oily fish, and turbot also works well in this recipe.

LINKS
> Serve with Pear, Walnut & Beetroot Salad, page 21.
> Substitute Rhubarb Syrup (page 36) or Lemon Syrup (page 82) for the honey. Both give an added dimension to fish.

Lavender Bread

I don't always have time to make this from scratch. However, most supermarkets sell packets of just-add-water bread mixes. The trick is to soak the lavender in 30ml of hot milk to rehydrate the flowers. This stops the bread from drying out as the lavender rehydrates and allows the flavour to merge throughout the bread. It also softens the petals, making the texture unnoticeable as you eat it. If you do have time to make this loaf from scratch, it is sensational – and is especially delicious as toast slathered in butter and honey.

Makes 1 large loaf
Prep time 40 minutes by hand,
20 minutes if using a food mixer
Cooking time 30–35 minutes
Suitable for freezing

2 tbsp culinary-grade dried lavender
30ml hot milk
750g strong plain white flour
7g sachet fast-action dried yeast
2 tsp salt
75g butter, cut into small pieces
330ml milk
1 tbsp caster sugar
100ml hot (but not boiling) water

1 Pop the lavender in a cup with the 30ml of hot milk and soak for about 15 minutes.

2 Put the flour, yeast and salt into a large bowl. Rub in the butter until it resembles fine breadcrumbs.

3 Pour the 330ml milk into a large measuring jug, stir in the sugar, hot water and the lavender and milk solution. The liquid should be just about hand temperature, and this warmth will help the bread rise.

4 Pour into the bowl of dry ingredients and mix until it forms a soft dough that leaves the sides of the bowl clean. Dust your work surface with flour, then tip the dough onto it. Knead the dough for about 10 minutes by hand, or use a dough hook on your mixer to do the same job. The dough should be stretchy and elastic.

5 Put into a lightly greased 1-litre tin and cover with a clean damp tea towel to rise for about 35 minutes.

6 Preheat the oven to 220°C/gas mark 7. Once the dough has risen, bake for 30 minutes, until fully risen and golden brown. Leave in the tin to cool.

7 Tip the loaf out onto a cooling rack and tap the base of the bread to check it is done. It should sound hollow.

TIP
● Leftover Lavender Bread makes a super bread pudding.

LINKS
> Serve with Rhubarb Jam, page 40.
> Use as the toast for Baked Goats Cheese and Lavender Honey on page 61.

Boozy Strawberries

These vodka and lavender-infused strawberries certainly have enough booziness to give you the impression of being much more indulgent than you actually are – perfect for those of us who want to feel as if we've had a decadent afternoon, but in reality simply can't. Aside from looking very pretty in the jam jars, these strawberries are also immensely practical. They take minutes to make, are easy to transport and can be eaten straight from the jar, which reduces washing up! The lids also help to keep the wasps away. To go a little more sophisticated and glam, tumble the strawberries out of the jars over meringue and pour on some cream. In summer, pop some fresh lavender petals and flowers in the jar, too.

Serves 4
Prep time 3 minutes

500g fresh strawberries and blueberries
1–2 tbsp vodka
2 tbsp Lavender Sugar **>**

1 Hull the strawberries. Halve any large ones and leave the bite-size ones whole.

2 Put these with the blueberries into 1 large jam jar (or 2 smaller ones) and sprinkle over the vodka and sugar. Don't be tempted to use too much; you just need a couple of tablespoons. Put the lid on the jar and shake gently.

3 Leave the fruit to infuse for 4–5 hours if possible. These are best served at room temperature to do the aroma justice. Just before serving, sprinkle a small amount of sugar over the top, and if you want you can pour cream directly into the jar, too.

TIPS & USES
● A versatile recipe that makes super portable picnic food as well as easy supper party fare.

● Almost any summer fruit works with this, so try nectarines, peaches, blueberries, kiwi fruit, ripe apricots and plums instead of strawberries and blueberries. A few rose petals look very pretty, too.

> ### LINKS
> **>** Lavender Sugar, page 58
> **>** Serve with Vanilla Ice Cream, page 118.
> **>** Use Plum Brandy (page 156) instead of vodka.

Lavender Shortbread

Shortbread: it's good no matter how you make it, but adding lavender to the mix sends it into the realms of dream food. The crunch, followed by the buttery melt in the mouth, is completed with a soft, aromatic lavender caress. As you can tell, I have a little love affair with shortbread. It's a treat with strawberries and cream, elevating a regular dessert into a top-notch offering. It is also one of my favourite gifts to give. Do make a large batch and freeze some dough; whipped straight from the freezer and baked, it's perfect in a food emergency. Just pop it in the oven and sail along as though nothing has ruffled your feathers.

Makes 35 x 40g biscuits or 27 biscuits and the base for 1 Rhubarb Pie (page 48)
Prep time 25 minutes
Cooking time 18–25 minutes
Suitable for freezing after step 2

200g Lavender Sugar >
500g butter
750g plain flour

1 Preheat the oven to 150°C/gas mark 2.

2 Sieve the lavender from the sugar and tip the spare petals back into the sugar jar. Cream the sugar with the butter until white and fluffy. This makes the shortbread light. Add the flour and mix well before turning out onto a work surface. If the mix is too crumbly and won't come together, add a teaspoon of water and remix. Roll out to about 1.5cm and cut the dough into the shapes you require.

3 Place the shortbread on a baking tray and bake for 18–20 minutes. Be warned: the colour at the end of cooking changes rapidly, so keep your eye on it.

4 Place on a wire rack to cool and sprinkle with a little more lavender sugar to serve.

LINKS
> Leaving out the lavender in this recipe makes the perfect base for a Rhubarb Pie (page 48). Cut away 300g of dough and line a 24cm quiche tin.
> Lavender Sugar, page 58
> Instantly change the flavour of this to Vanilla Shortbread or Cardamom Shortbread (which goes wonderfully with coffee) just by swapping the sugar: pages 108 and 226.

TIPS & USES
● Make extra dough and freeze it as a base to make a pie.

● Although some people like to see the lavender in the shortbread, I prefer mine invisible. I do, however, leave the lavender in as I sprinkle the sugar over the pieces at the end. This way you can easily dust off the petals.

Chocolate Cupcakes with Lavender Cream

A soft, moist, rich chocolate sponge with a sweet, fresh lavender cream inside, this cupcake is lifted by lavender's minty tones. Serve it drizzled with milk chocolate and a scattering of lavender petals. Be sure to use lavender with a closed bud to infuse your cream because open petals have lost most of the essential oils responsible for the flavour. For the prettiest colour, use old-fashioned cottage garden lavender such as Hidcote.

Makes 24
Prep time 1 day to infuse the lavender into the cream and 20 minutes to prep
Cooking time 20 minutes
Suitable for freezing At step 6

250g butter
250g Lavender Sugar >
4 large eggs
200g self-raising flour
1 level tsp baking powder
50g cocoa powder

For the filling
12 heads of fresh lavender
600ml double cream
100g milk chocolate, for drizzling

TIPS & USES

● The cupcakes are at their most delicious served at room temperature. Best eaten on the same day they're made.

● Double the recipe and make a spare large one of these at the same time as making cupcakes. Just divide the mixture between two 23cm diameter cake tins and bake for 25–30 minutes. Sandwich together with the lavender cream. Trust me: it will come in handy!

● If you'd like your cupcakes a lavender colour, then use a violet concentrated icing gel food colour paste and follow the recommended instructions to turn your cream a lovely shade of lavender.

1 Put the lavender for the filling into the cream and leave to infuse for 24 hours or longer for a stronger flavour. If you're in a hurry, double the lavender, gently bruise the flowers between your fingers and leave out of the fridge for 2–3 hours.

2 Preheat the oven to 180°C/gas mark 4.

3 Beat together the butter and sugar well until white and fluffy. Beat the eggs and add them gradually to the creamed mixture. A few tablespoons of flour (use this from the allocated 200g) added in before you add the eggs will prevent the batter from curdling. (It's not the end of the world if it does curdle; just keep going – the flour will bring it all together again when it's added.)

4 Sift the flour, baking powder and cocoa powder into the creamed mixture. Mix well.

5 Spoon the mixture into 24 large cupcake cases. Bake in the oven for 20–25 minutes until firm to the touch. Transfer to a wire rack to cool. They must be absolutely cool before you add the cream.

6 Strain the cream and whip to a firm consistency. Cut out a slice from the top of each cupcake to make a hollow.

7 Dollop a tablespoon of cream into each indentation. Cut the remaining piece of cake in half and place on top of the cream to give an old-fashioned butterfly-cake effect.

8 Melt the chocolate in a heatproof bowl over a pan of hot water, then trickle it over the cakes. Scatter with open lavender flowers just before serving.

LINKS
> Lavender Sugar: page 58
> Chocolate Truffle Ganache,
  page 212: use any leftover ganache
  to decorate the tops.

Lavender & Lemon Cake

My get-ahead trick with this cake is always to make two. It stashes in the freezer beautifully. I decorate it while it's still frozen so I can have it waiting for a teatime treat – for when we get in from wherever we've been – and still look like I've slaved for hours. The combination of lavender and lemon is nothing less than stunning.

Serves 6–8
Prep time 20 minutes
Cooking time 45 minutes
Suitable for freezing

For the cake
2 large eggs
175g Lavender Sugar **>** (sifted)
160g soft butter or margarine
Grated zest of 1 lemon
175g sifted self-raising flour
125ml milk
Pinch of sea salt

For the icing
Juice of 2 lemons
1 drop of red food colouring
1 drop of blue food colouring
8–10 tbsp icing sugar

To drizzle
3 tbsp Lemon Syrup **>**
OR
If you don't have any Lemon Syrup to
  hand, use the juice of 1 lemon plus
  3 tsp lemon juice

To decorate
Lavender flowers and edible iced flowers

1 Preheat the oven to 180°C/gas mark 4). Line the bottom of a well-oiled 23cm x 13cm x 8cm loaf tin with baking parchment.

2 Put the eggs and sugar in a bowl and mix with an electric hand mixer for 2 minutes, scraping the sides down once with a spatula to make sure you've got all the mix in. Add the butter and grated zest and mix; the batter will look rather like mayonnaise.

3 Add the flour, milk and salt, and mix gently until the batter is smooth in texture and even in colour. Go easy with the mixing; it's important not to overbeat or the cake will be tough.

4 Spoon the cake mixture into the tin and bake for 45 minutes until golden brown on top and firm to the touch. Remove from the oven and stand the tin on a cooling rack.

5 While the cake is still warm, prick it all over with a cocktail stick and gently pour the syrup over it until it has been completely absorbed.

6 I love to serve this cake plain at this point and just top it with a little more icing sugar. If you prefer to ice it, then once the cake is completely cold, mix together all the icing ingredients and pour over the cake before decorating it with the flowers.

LINKS
> Lavender Sugar, page 58
> Lemon Syrup makes a seriously lemony drizzle for this cake: page 82.
> Replace the Lavender Sugar with Cardamom Sugar (page 226) to make a Cardamom & Lemon Cake.

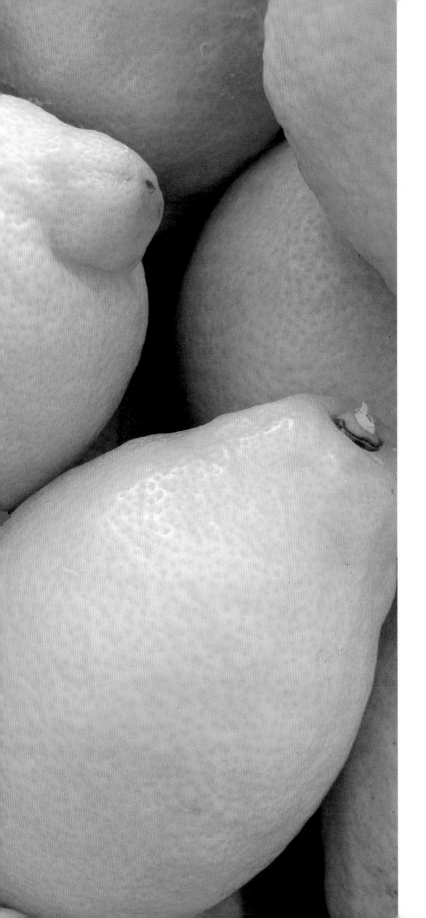

Lemon

*Zesty, zingy, fresh
bright-sunshine
yellow lemons.
Cheek-puckering,
eye-wincing, sour,
sharp, mouthwatering,
gazillion-taste-buds-
clanging lemons.*

*Paired with soft folds
of cream and sugar,
this sharp citrus fruit
becomes a love affair,
while in a salad
dressing it adds a
knock-out, ding-dong,
next-round-please
wallop of freshness.
Whichever way you
serve it, lemon is
the absolute key to
the contrast that gives
food a full-powered
flavour punch.*

Lemon Syrup

You only have to mention homemade lemonade to elicit envious smiles from your girlfriends. Why? Because they're torn between joining you and leaving in disgust at your fantastical domesticity! Yet this syrup is as magical as the one Alice in Wonderland drank. One sip and you're transformed into everything that years of vintage crockery-collecting represents. No need for an antidote: just pull up a pretty cushioned chair, add a drop of gin and ply them with a friendship-winning White Rabbit Cocktail (page 85). They'll soon come round!

Makes 1 litre
Prep time 25 minutes
Cooking time 5 minutes

Zest and juice of 7 lemons
500ml water
500g caster sugar

1 Put all the ingredients into a pan over a low heat and gently dissolve the sugar.

2 Bring to the boil and boil rapidly for 3–4 minutes. Allow the liquid to become still and scoop off any foam. The syrup should have thickened slightly and become more viscous. If it is not, then return it to the boil for another minute. It is better to be on the under- than the over-side of syrupy. If you overdo it, you'll end up with a bottle full of jelly!

3 Decant the liquid into a sterilised bottle, and dilute with water to taste. It will keep in the fridge for up to 4 weeks.

TIP
● This recipe works with plums; however, you'll need to add about 250ml of water to make plum syrup.

LINKS
> Lemon Syrup links to most recipes in this chapter.
> Use to make another version of the Ginger von Tease cocktail on page 17.
> Try it in place of Elderflower & Rose Syrup in Lime & Elderflower Salad Dressing (page 18) and Elderflower & Lime Macaroons (page 30).
> To make a delicious lemon sorbet, follow the recipe for Elderflower Sorbet on page 22, substituting the Lemon Syrup for the Elderflower & Rose. And for a touch of spice, use ginger beer instead of bitter lemon.
> Use instead of Elderflower & Rose Syrup in Baked Trout with Chilli & Elderflower, page 25.
> Try it in place of Elderflower & Rose Syrup in the jelly recipe on page 29.
> Swap for Rhubarb Syrup in Mackerel & Rhubarb Pasta/Pâté, page 43.
> Use as the drizzle in the Lemon Cake, page 105.

LEMON DRIZZLE CREAM POTS

To make supersonic, zesty Lemon Drizzle Cream Pots for six, simply follow the recipe for Rhubarb Fool on page 47, but omit the rhubarb and use 1 lemon, sliced, in place of the mixed fruit. Whip 3 tbsp icing sugar into 500ml double cream. Divide the slices of lemon among 6 glasses. Break the meringues into a bowl and pour on 120ml of Lemon Syrup, then mix in the whipped cream. Divide the creamy meringue mixture among the glasses and serve.

White Rabbit Cocktail

In Alice in Wonderland, *the White Rabbit rushes around with his watch, muttering about how he will be late. There is something familiar about this poor chap. I have a friend (who shall remain unnamed) who does a great impression of him. This superb cocktail is not only made in a blink of an eye, but is guaranteed to make this sort of person stop, put down the watch and enjoy a tangy, stimulating and refreshing cocktail before he remembers where he should be. By the second one, he won't care anymore!*

1 part gin
2 parts Lemon Syrup **>**
2 parts tonic

1 Mix all the ingredients in a cocktail glass over ice and serve.

St Clement's Cocktail

'Oranges and lemons,' said the bells of St Clement's – a fabulous combination of the orange in the Cointreau and the lemon, which sits over the top. Hopefully you won't hear bells if you drink too many!

1 part Cointreau
2 parts Lemon Syrup **>**
2 parts tonic

1 Mix all the ingredients in a cocktail glass over ice and serve.

> **LINK**
> **>** Lemon Syrup, page 82

Lemon & Chilli Oysters

Seductive, sophisticated and somehow decadent, I love the saltiness of oysters, the soft flesh slipping effortlessly down my throat, finished with a sip of Champagne. It's no accident that they go so well together – but I find some things can still be improved upon. In this dish, the saltiness of oysters is exaggerated by the sugar and lemony tang in this recipe, and it's such a simple, yet elegant, starter.

Serves 4
Prep time 5 minutes

1 medium shallot,
  finely chopped
1 red chilli, sliced
12 oysters, opened
50ml Lemon Syrup **>**
Chives, to scatter

1 Scatter the shallots and chilli over the oysters.

2 Drizzle with Lemon Syrup, scatter with chives and serve them immediately on a bed of ice.

> **LINKS**
> **>** Substitute Elderflower & Rose Syrup (page 14) for the Lemon Syrup.
> **>** Lemon Syrup, page 82

Two-for-one Asparagus

Elegant, slender, juicy… British asparagus is made all the more desirable by the short May/June season and I just can't get enough of it. These long, green spears marry well with sweet lemon syrup and salty anchovies, with a side kick of sour from the capers – a terrific agreement of flavours. It's so versatile you can play with the method; toss them through warm couscous for a warm summer salad (which makes a first-class packed lunch with any leftover), or grill the ingredients and throw them over a toasted panini. Alternatively, the same ingredients are used in a classic quiche, cooked with a crumbly, all-butter short pastry and served with roasted tomatoes – it's divine. The asparagus slices make a delectable drinks nibble.

Both recipes serve 6–8
Prep time 10 minutes
Cooking time Quiche & Slice: both
25–30 minutes; Couscous: 5 minutes
Suitable for freezing Only the quiche

Base ingredients for both recipes
A large bunch of asparagus
40g fresh grated Parmesan
2 tbsp capers
30g anchovies in olive oil, drained
Zest of 2 unwaxed lemons (reserve the
   juice for the third recipe)

Asparagus, Anchovy & Parmesan Quiche
Base ingredients, plus:
3 eggs, beaten
140ml semi-skimmed milk
375g pack ready-roll shortcrust pastry

Lemon & Asparagus Couscous
Base ingredients, plus:
500g couscous
50g butter
30ml Lemon or
   Elderflower & Rose Syrup **>**
A handful of parsley

LINKS
> Use Elderflower & Rose Syrup
  instead of Lemon Syrup: page 14.
> Lemon Syrup, page 82

Asparagus, Anchovy & Parmesan Quiche

1 Preheat the oven to 180°C/gas mark 4.

2 Roll out the pastry and line a 26cm quiche dish. Blind-bake the pasty for 15 minutes using baking parchment and baking beans. Remove the paper, cut the asparagus to fit and arrange as you find attractive. Scatter with the Parmesan and capers, and add anchovies and zest.

3 In a separate bowl, beat the eggs and milk and pour into the dish. Bake for 25–30 minutes until it has risen and is a golden colour.

Lemon & Asparagus Couscous

1 Prepare the couscous according to the packet instructions. Stir in the lemon zest, butter, and Parmesan.

2 Discard 2.5cm of each asparagus base and place the stems on a baking tray. Lay slivers of anchovies between the spears and drizzle any olive oil left in the anchovy can over the spears.

3 Grill for about 2–3 minutes until slightly firm.

4 Add the grilled asparagus to the couscous, drench with Lemon Syrup and capers and mix lightly. Serve hot or cold and scatter with parsley.

Chicken & Lemon Rice Soup

Soup isn't the first thing that springs to mind as a summer dish, but to me, lemony chicken rice soup is sunshine in a bowl. I prefer my bowl to be full of rice and vegetables rather than with a lot of liquid, but you can adjust that according to your taste.

Serves 4
Prep time 10 minutes
Cooking time 10–12 minutes
Suitable for freezing

2 tbsp olive oil
2 garlic cloves, peeled and finely chopped
3 celery stems, sliced
2 medium yellow courgettes, sliced
3 bay leaves
500g cooked chicken (best as leftovers
   from a roast, but 2 chicken breasts
   are fine, too)
Lemon Syrup **>** OR 2 tbsp caster sugar
1.5 litres chicken stock
85g basmati rice
Pinch of salt
Juice of 2 lemons
1 fresh chilli, finely chopped

1 Heat the oil in a heavy-based saucepan and sauté the garlic cloves, celery and courgettes for 3–4 minutes, or until just soft.

2 Add the bay leaves, chicken, syrup or sugar, stock and rice to the pan. Bring to the boil, cover and simmer for 10 minutes. Don't be tempted to overdo the rice; it will keep cooking for another few minutes, so having it just underdone will give the best result.

3 Season with the salt, add the lemon juice and serve scattered with the finely chopped fresh chilli.

LINKS
> Lemon Syrup, page 82
> Use leftover Lemon Roast Chicken (page 101).

Lemon Clams

This dish is super-quick. It's also rather grown-up. It makes a spontaneous lunch, so when you spot these beauties at the market, grab the opportunity. I urge you to buy them. Don't stare at them wondering what to do with them; just come home with your seaside treasure, a bottle of Chablis and a French stick and knock this up in a jiffy. They are fabulous – just fabulous!

Serves 2
Prep time 5 minutes
Cooking time 5 minutes

15ml rapeseed or olive oil
1 onion (or a couple of shallots)
20 clams
50ml Lemon Syrup **>**
60ml water
1 chilli (finely chopped), fresh chopped
   dill and lemon wedges, to serve

1 In a heavy-based saucepan, add the rapeseed oil and sauté the onion over a medium heat. Drop in the clams and add the Lemon Syrup and water. Cover and bring to a high heat.

2 Steam the clams for about 4 minutes. Discard any that have not opened.

3 Scatter with chilli and dill and serve with a wedge of lemon.

LINK
> Lemon Syrup, page 82

Double Cook: Pork Knuckle Terrine & Lemon Pork Risotto

By cooking three gammon hocks together you can get prepped for a terrific terrine for a starter or lunch dish as well as an outstanding risotto for supper.

Pork Knuckle Terrine

Over the years I've noticed that men especially enjoy the rugged texture of sweet, fragrant pork terrine: the salted, pink, dense meat just seems to appeal to the male palate. I always serve this with a sweet relish such as Spiced Tomato Jam. The easiest way to cook hocks is in a slow cooker; they just bubble away all day.

Serves 4–6
Prep time 30 minutes
Cooking time 6 hours
Suitable for freezing

3 pork gammon hocks on the bone
   (normally about 3 in total)
1 tbsp honey
4 tbsp Lemon Syrup >
6 cloves
6 cardamom pods
6 juniper berries
2 star anise
4 sprigs fresh tarragon
Small pinch of salt

LINKS

> Lemon Syrup, page 82
> Spiced Tomato Jam, page 128
> Serve with Soda Bread, page 196.

1 Put the first 7 ingredients in a very large pan or slow cooker and cover the hocks with cold water. Cook on a very low heat or on the low setting for 8 hours (or overnight). Allow to cool for about 1 hour or so; it is important not to allow it to cook completely.

2 Once the meat has cooled, strip off the pink gammon, ensuring no tendons make it into the bowl by mistake. I do this in the sink over a couple of plastic shopping bags: the least messy way to do it and the birds love the leftover fat in midwinter! You should end up with about 800g of meat, give or take a few grams. The stock is very important to the next recipe, so strain it into a large container and pop it in the fridge.

3 Split the meat into 2 lots. Put 400g into a container and put this in the fridge; leave the other 400g in the bowl. I allow 100g per person as a portion for the terrine, so 400g is about right for 4 starters.

4 Chop about 4 sprigs of tarragon finely, discarding any tough stems. Add this and a small pinch of salt to the mix. Use your fingers to break up the meat, then mix in the herbs well. If it looks a little dry, add 2–3 tablespoons of the reserved stock in the fridge to moisten and stir in the lemon zest.

5 Push the mixture into either one large mould or 4 small moulds (a muffin tray will do). Place cling film over the top and return the mould to the fridge with weights on top to set for a minimum of 4 hours. Alternatively, you can freeze them at this point.

Lemon Pork Risotto

The other dish that inspired this combination – from Le Brasserie Blanc, Oxford – uses up any leftover stock from the Pork Knuckle Terrine to create an equally delicious risotto. This is my own version. It is wonderfully comforting and easy to make with a rich, salty Parmesan, soft, flavoursome ham hock and tarragon.

Serves 4
Prep time 10 minutes
Cooking time 25–30 minutes

2 tbsp rapeseed oil
2 banana shallots, finely chopped
1 garlic clove, finely chopped
60g unsalted butter
500g arborio rice
1100ml leftover pork stock
   (from Pork Knuckle Terrine **>**)
2 bay leaves
Juice and zest from 2 lemons
5 tbsp Plum Brandy **>**
4 sprigs tarragon, finely chopped
60g grated Parmesan
400g roughly chopped ham hock
Slices of lemon, to garnish

1 Heat the oil in a large, heavy-based saucepan and sauté the shallots and garlic over a medium heat. Add the butter and, when melted, add in the rice and bay leaves. Stir well, making sure each grain is covered in butter.

2 Add the pork stock, one ladle at a time. Keeping the hob on a medium heat, stir in each ladle with a wooden spoon and only add the next one when the previous one has been absorbed. Use up about two-thirds of the stock in this way; the process takes about 20 minutes. Be contemplative and relaxed about this, and resist the temptation to run off and do other jobs in between ladles. Otherwise you'll ruin the dish because it catches quickly!

3 Pour in the rest of the stock, pop the lid on and simmer very gently for about 15 minutes. Stir regularly to check that it doesn't stick, until the stock is fully absorbed and the rice is cooked and has lost its bite. Add the lemon juice, zest and brandy and give a final mix. Cook for another couple of minutes.

4 Stir in the chopped tarragon, Parmesan and the ham hock. Cover and allow to sit for another minute or two to warm up. Serve with slices of lemon. A chutney to accompany is a must!

LINKS
> Instead of the 400g of ham hock used in this recipe, substitute the same quantity of cooked Lavender Chicken (page 65).
> Plum Brandy, page 156

Hot or Cold Lemon Chicken Rice Salad

It doesn't take much to assemble this chicken salad. It's filling, zesty and makes a packed lunch the whole office will be envious of the next day. You can make this hot if you prefer: just sauté some onions, transfer the hot rice straight into the pan and follow the method below. I do love this recipe's versatility!

Serves 4–6
Prep time 20 minutes

250g basmati rice
  (weighed before cooking)
400g cooked Lemon Roast Chicken **>**
200g cooked sweetcorn (drained weight)
Handful of fresh dill or basil and mint
1 x 30g tin anchovies in olive oil,
  thinly chopped
4–5 tbsp capers, sliced in half
1 red chilli, finely chopped
Salt and black pepper to taste
Slices of lemon, to garnish

For the Lemon Salad Dressing
45ml Lemon Syrup **>**
30ml light olive oil
1 tbsp English mustard

1 Cook the rice according to the packet instructions. Drain it in a colander, then run the colander under a cold tap for 1 minute. This stops the rice from continuing to cook and it will stay firm and light.

2 Shred the chicken and add it to the rice in a bowl. Mix well and add the sweetcorn, chopped dill, anchovies, capers, chilli and season to taste.

3 To make the salad dressing, combine all the ingredients in a jam jar and shake vigorously for 1 minute. Do make sure the lid is on firmly before shaking or you will have a comedy moment!

4 Drizzle with the salad dressing and mix well.

LINKS
> Change the flavour of the salad dressing by using Elderflower & Rose Syrup instead of Lemon Syrup, page 14…
> …or use Lime & Elderflower Salad Dressing (page 18) instead of Lemon Dressing.
> Substitute Lavender Baked Salmon for the chicken: page 68.
> Lemon Syrup, page 82
> Lemon Roast Chicken, page 101.

Lemon Roast Chicken

No foodie is without his or her favourite roast chicken recipe. All great chefs have a version, and this is mine. Aside from being seriously easy and wonderful to eat (it can be in the oven in just ten minutes), it's great to wrap in foil straight out of the oven and throw into the boot of the car with a basket of bread rolls, a blanket and a bottle of lemonade for an instant, self-assembled Sunday afternoon picnic. Don't forget the napkins!

Serves 6
Prep time 12 minutes
Cooking time 1 hour 30 minutes
Suitable for freezing

2 bay leaves
5–6 garlic cloves, peeled
Zest and juice of 2 lemons
1 large chicken (about 1.6kg)
3 tbsp olive or rapeseed oil
2 tsp good-quality sea salt
1 large glass (240ml) white wine
½ tsp sugar
2 tbsp cornflour
2–3 tbsp single cream (optional)
Chopped chives, to garnish

TIP
● Never roast just one chicken; always do two. That way you use the same oven heat and are prepped, ready for half a dozen other things you can make with chicken.

LINKS
> Chicken & Lemon Rice Soup, page 90
> Hot or Cold Lemon Chicken Rice Salad, page 98
> Caraway & Lemon Chicken Pasties, page 191

1 Preheat the oven to 240°C/gas mark 9. Put the bay leaves, garlic and lemon zest inside the chicken's cavity; also put some under the breast skin. Place it in a roasting pan, drizzle with the oil and rub it in, then sprinkle salt over the top of the chicken.

2 Reduce the oven temperature to 200°C/gas 6 and cook for 1 hour.

3 Baste the chicken with the juices, then add the wine to the pan. After 20 more minutes in the oven, check to see that the chicken is cooked by inserting a skewer in the thigh and making sure the juices run clear. If they're still pink, return the bird to the oven for 10 more minutes and repeat the test.

4 Remove the chicken from the pan and set to one side to rest. A few minutes' rest allows the meat to relax: it will be much more tender as a result. In the meantime, make the gravy. Strain the liquid from the roasting pan into a gravy separator and discard the fat, before returning the juice to the pan. Over a medium heat add the lemon juice and stir in the sugar. Taste here, and add more sugar, salt or water according to your preference.

5 Make the cornflour into a watery paste by adding a few drops of water at a time and mixing well. Add this to the chicken juices while stirring all the time to thicken the sauce. Pop the pan onto the hob, bring the heat up gently and keep stirring, but don't quite boil. Cook this through for a minute or so to get a smooth gravy. For a more voluptuous sauce, stir in 2–3 tablespoons of cream just before serving.

6 Slice the meat and cover in this lemon-infused gravy. Scatter with chopped chives as you serve.

Lemon Polenta Savoury Muffins

Those of us who are short on time but still want to produce something from the kitchen should look no further than the muffin. These are loaded with flavour and texture, and pack a generous lemony/herby bite. What's more, there's very little washing up to do! I love to pair these with a hot soup as a packed lunch – and they really can cheer you up served warm from the oven on a rainy day. If you want to freeze them, don't hang about: get them straight in the freezer because they lose their freshness quickly.

Makes 20
Prep time 10 minutes
Cooking time 25 minutes
Suitable for freezing

325g plain flour
200g instant polenta
2 tsp baking powder
1 tsp bicarbonate of soda
125g butter (soft)
80ml rapeseed or olive oil
3 large eggs
284ml buttermilk (standard pot size)
A handful of fresh mixed chopped
   herbs: parsley, basil, dill, marjoram
Zest and juice of 2 lemons
45ml Lemon Syrup **>**
1 tbsp sea salt flakes
A good grinding of cracked
   black pepper

TIP
● Unless you're using a silicone muffin tray (which I recommend), use paper muffin cases.

1 Preheat the oven to 190°C/gas mark 5.

2 In a large bowl, stir together the flour, polenta, baking powder and bicarbonate of soda. Using a hand mixer on a low speed, add the butter and oil, mixing until the batter resembles breadcrumbs.

3 Add the eggs, buttermilk, herbs, lemon zest and juice and Lemon Syrup. Mix for another minute or so. Don't over-mix.

4 Spoon the batter up to almost the top of each hole of the muffin tins. Sprinkle the sea salt flakes and cracked black pepper over the top of each. Bake until golden – about 20–25 minutes. The muffins are done when they are golden brown and spring back to the touch. Serve warm with butter.

LINK
> Lemon Syrup, page 82

Lemon Cake

I sent this recipe to Julia, one of my testers. When I spoke to her the following week she said she had made it six times since – it really is that good! I think if I had one bit of advice about making this cake, it would be to make two at the same time.

Serves 8
Prep time 20 minutes
Cooking time 35 minutes
Suitable for freezing
Before drizzling the syrup

200g caster sugar
200g unsalted butter,
  cubed and softened
Finely grated zest of 2 lemons
3 medium eggs, beaten,
  at room temperature
200g self-raising flour
80ml Lemon Syrup **>**
  OR Lavender & Lemon Syrup **>**

LINKS
> Lavender & Lemon Syrup, page 62
> Lemon Syrup, page 82
> Use any of the following sugars for
  a different flavour: Lavender Sugar
  (page 58), Cardamom Sugar (page
  226), Orange & Clove (page 245).

---

1 Preheat the oven to 180°C/gas mark 4. Grease a 20cm, round springform cake tin and line the base with a disc of baking parchment.

2 Put the sugar, softened butter and lemon zest in a mixing bowl and beat with a wooden spoon or an electric hand mixer. The result should be pale in colour, with a really light and fluffy texture. Putting in the lemon zest when you cream the butter and sugar helps to release the oils in the zest, which results in a much more lemony sponge.

3 Now start adding the beaten eggs, which should be at roughly the same temperature as the butter and sugar. Add them in stages, beating after each addition. If the mixture looks like it's going to curdle, add 1 tablespoon of flour. Finally, fold in the flour. You will be left with a really thick mixture, but this is what you want for a dense sponge.

4 Spoon the mixture into your prepared tin and bake for 35–45 minutes until the cake shrinks away from the side. Test it with a skewer to see if the mixture is cooked in the centre; it should come out clean. If not, put it back in the oven for a few minutes and test again. Remove from the oven and, if it is done, prick all over with a cocktail stick about 20 times.

5 Drizzle the lemon syrup over the cake slowly, waiting a few moments before adding more, so it all sinks in. It should leave a crust on the cake. Remove from the tin and transfer to a wire rack to cool.

TIP
● You can use about half of this cake as the base to make the Hot Tipover Trifle on page 52.

Vanilla

If vanilla were an instrument, it would be a harp, its notes singing out above the rest of the orchestra, like an angel's voice, singularly noticeable for its utter beauty.

To me, vanilla is how 'beautiful' tastes. With its deep, dark, sticky-sweet, fragrant, gentle notes, it accentuates, complements and harmonises, while still sitting high.

Vanilla Sugar

There are few things in life I couldn't live without. In domestic terms, vanilla sugar is one of them. It is the backbone of most of my baking. What prevents most people from making a huge pot of vanilla sugar is the sheer cost, so my advice is to build the pot slowly. Buy one good-quality vanilla pod every now and then. The sugar preserves them and they infuse flavour for years. I know some people who ask for pods as birthday presents! And it's worth it, because the sugar really is a treat to use and can make all the difference to food.

Makes 1 large 2kg pot
Prep time Less than a minute!

4–5 vanilla pods
2kg caster sugar

1 Pop the vanilla pods in a large jar and cover with caster sugar. Seal well.

2 Leave to infuse for 3–4 weeks or longer.

TIP
● Each time you use any sugar, replace with more sugar and shake the jar well to mix the flavour and keep the vanilla taste throughout. This way you always have vanilla sugar on hand.

LINKS
> Vanilla Sugar links to many recipes in this chapter.
> Use to add an extra dimension to Rhubarb Syrup, page 36.
> Use in place of Cardamom Sugar in 100mph Rhubarb & Cardamom Batter Cake, page 55.
> Use instead of Lavender Sugar in Lavender Shortbread, page 75, and in place of caster sugar in Chocolate Cookie Mix, page 206.

Vanilla Vinegar

This vinegar takes about three minutes to make. Although it does need storing for at least two weeks before using, it's on my list of emergency gifts. After all, it's not as though you can pick it up in the local supermarket. The sweet vanilla bursts through, adding top notes to even the most mundane salad dressing.

Makes 500ml
Prep time 3 minutes

1 whole vanilla bean
500ml good-quality white-wine or rice vinegar

1 Cut the vanilla pod in half lengthwise and put the pieces into a clean, 500ml bottle (I keep pretty used bottles for just this purpose).

2 Using a funnel, pour the vinegar into the bottle, seal it and then shake for 1–2 minutes. Label and date the bottle.

3 To extract the maximum amount of vanilla flavour, shake the bottle twice a day for a week or two (although to be fair, when I've forgotten to do this it really hasn't made an awful lot of difference). You can use it after a fortnight, but it is best after 3–4 weeks.

TIPS & USES
● The longer this sits, the better the flavour.

● As you use it, top up the bottle with a little more vinegar.

● This vinegar adds another flavour dimension to anything you use it in. Try it when making mayonnaise or hollandaise sauce, for example.

● Make it using balsamic vinegar. Wonderful!

LINKS
> Use it to make Rhubarb Pavlova, page 44.
> Broccoli with Hot Vanilla Vinaigrette, page 113

Vanilla Vodka

You can buy flavoured vodkas, but believe me: this is so much nicer and more vanilla-y. I love this in cocktails and to give as a gift with a cocktail recipe attached to the bottle, but it also infuses the most delightful flavours into Christmas puddings – if you can bear to pour it in the pudding rather than into a cocktail glass!

Makes 1 x 75cl bottle
Prep time 2 minutes – or more if you drink some!

75cl vodka
3 vanilla pods
250g Vanilla Sugar >
2 tsp of edible glitter (optional)

1 Put all the ingredients into a sterile glass bottle and seal. Shake well.

2 Shake several times a day over the course of a week and the sugar will dissolve to leave you with a beautiful clear liqueur with vanilla flecks.

Vanilla White Russian

Serves 1
Prep time 2 minutes

50ml Vanilla Vodka >
25ml coffee liqueur
25ml single cream
Cocoa powder, for dusting

Fill a shaker (or a jam jar if you don't have one) two-thirds full of ice. Add a large (50ml) shot of Vanilla Vodka and a shot of Kahlua or other coffee liqueur. Shake and strain into an ice-filled glass. Pour a small shot of single cream over the top – you get it to sit on top by pouring it over the back of a spoon. Finish with a dusting of cocoa powder.

TIP
● You can use Baileys instead of cream.

LINK
> Vanilla Sugar, page 108

Broccoli with Hot Vanilla Vinaigrette

This might sound like one of the most bizarre recipes ever, but trust me: it just works. It tastes delicious and looks amazing and is exceedingly quick to make. It is also excellent served cold as a salad, but I find that it accompanies roast chicken particularly well.

Makes 4
Prep time 5 minutes
Cooking time 4 minutes

1 large head of broccoli, cut into florets
   (or enough purple-sprouting broccoli
   for 4 people)
40g butter
50ml Vanilla Vinegar **>**
1 tbsp English mustard
Pinch of salt
40g caster sugar
Seeds from half a pomegranate
3–4 tbsp pine nuts

1 Drop the broccoli into a pan of boiling water and cook for 3–4 minutes.

2 In the meantime, melt the butter in a pan, add the vanilla vinegar and stir in the English mustard. Gently whisk so that it forms an emulsion, season with a little salt and then add the sugar.

3 Drain the broccoli and put it into a serving dish. Immediately pour the dressing over the cooked broccoli, tumble over the pomegranate seeds and pine nuts and serve immediately.

TIP
● Serve the sauce alone over baked trout or as a dressing for potato salad with plenty of chives.

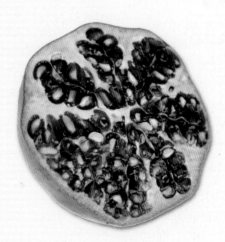

LINK
> Vanilla Vinegar, page 109

Instant Vanilla Pancake Mix

There are moments when you need to walk in the door and make something without any fuss: something fast, delicious and pleasing to all. Whether you've just invited extra children home for tea, or you've come in from an afternoon in the garden, pancakes are universally welcome and instant – especially if you've got your mix already prepped.

Makes 8 batches
  (1 batch makes 6 pancakes)
Prep time 5 minutes
Cooking time 10 minutes

For the mix
1kg flour
200g Vanilla Sugar >
8 tsp baking powder
4 tsp mixed spice
4 tsp sea salt

To make 1 batch of pancakes
150g pancake mix
240ml semi-skimmed milk
2 eggs
1 tbsp vegetable or rapeseed oil
  per pancake, for frying

1 Sieve all the mix ingredients together and really mix well. Transfer into a large, clean, airtight jar.

2 Put the 150g of pancake mix into a bowl; add the milk and 2 eggs. Whisk.

3 Heat the oil in a frying pan. Using a jug, pour in the batter to whatever size/thickness you want and roll the pan gently to ensure even coverage. Turn the heat down to low and cook for 1 minute. Turn the pancake over (feel free to do a fancy flip once you've made sure the pancake isn't stuck!) Cook the opposite side and serve.

TIPS & USES
● I serve my pancakes with lashings of maple syrup and sautéed apples in butter topped with ice cream.

● If you have time, allow the pancake mix to stand for a few minutes before cooking; this seems to make a smoother pancake.

LINKS
> Any of the syrups or sugar flavours throughout this book make superb accompaniments; see Elderflower & Rose Syrup, page 14; Rhubarb Syrup, page 36; Lavender Sugar, page 58; Lavender & Lemon Syrup, page 62; Lemon Syrup, page 82; Cardamom Sugar, page 226; or Orange & Clove Sugar, page 245.
> Vanilla Sugar, page 108

Vanilla, Mango & Chilli Pork

The initial idea might seem a little strange, but this dish has all the foundations of traditional sweet-and-sour pork, but with a sophisticated twist. To me, combining flavours is like playing a musical chord – the notes need to harmonise – and this pork recipe does just that. The vanilla sits in the mid-tones, while the mango provides a higher note. The fruit also creates a soft, contrasting texture, and the chilli is the kick at the end. But all you really need to know is that is quite simply delicious. Do try it.

Serves 4
Prep time 10 minutes
Cooking time 15 minutes

1 vanilla pod, split lengthways
  (or 1 tbsp vanilla paste)
2–3 tbsp toasted sesame oil
2 shallots, finely chopped
1kg pork fillet steak, cubed
½ tsp chilli powder
2 tbsp Vanilla Vodka **>**
1 tbsp fish sauce
1 fresh chilli, chopped
2 fresh ripe mangos, cut into 2.5cm
  cubes, plus extra for garnish
1 tsp fine sea salt
50ml single cream
Fresh coriander or basil, to serve

1 Slice the vanilla pods down the middle to release the vanilla flavour.

2 Heat the oil in a wok or large frying pan and sauté the chopped shallots for a couple of minutes before adding the pork, split vanilla and chilli powder. Don't drop all the pork in the pan at once; add in a handful at a time, stir and allow the heat to catch up before adding the next handful. As you stir-fry the pork, allow it to catch a little to caramelise – but don't burn it. Keep the heat hot, but not on too high. Keep stirring all the while. Add the Vanilla Vodka and fish sauce, then add the fresh chopped chillies.

3 After about 4 minutes add half the cubed mango. Continue to stir and move the pork around the wok for another 5–6 minutes until the meat is cooked. Check by picking out a small piece and cutting into the middle. If it's pink, return it to the pan and continue cooking for another minute or so.

4 Add the salt and cream and stir to mix through the juices.

5 Serve on a bed of warm rice, scattered with more fresh mango, chilli and fresh coriander or basil.

TIPS & USES
● Ideal for a fast dinner party dish for four or lunch with friends.

● It also makes a super cold salad with rice for a packed lunch.

LINK
> Vanilla Vodka, page 110

Vanilla Custard

The thing about this custard is that with one recipe you can swap and change it accordingly. In summer, make lavender custard, or in December make a festive orange and clove one. What I do recommend to be really prepped is that you make twice the amount here and simply tip half into an ice-cream maker and hey presto! like magic, you have homemade ice cream in the freezer of whatever flavour of custard you've made – and all for no extra time, effort or washing up. Genius, even if I do say so myself!

Serves 6
Makes 750ml
Prep time 5 minutes
Cooking time 15–20 minutes

500ml full-fat milk
200ml double cream
5 egg yolks
100g Vanilla Sugar **>**

1 Put the milk, cream, egg yolks and sugar in a heavy-based saucepan and stir over a moderate heat. Keep moving the liquid using a whisk.

2 Keep stirring as the custard thickens. This can take 10–15 minutes so take your time and don't be tempted to heat it quickly (you'll get scrambled eggs!). The mixture will thicken. When the custard easily coats the back of a spoon, remove it from the heat.

3 Serve hot or cold.

TIPS & USES
● For a stronger vanilla flavour, add 5 drops of pure vanilla essence.

● In order to turn this recipe into ice cream, follow the instructions in step 4 for Rhubarb & Custard Ice Cream on page 51.

LINKS
> Change the base flavour: use Lavender Sugar (page 58), Cardamom Sugar (page 226) or Orange & Clove Sugar (page 245) instead of Vanilla Sugar.
> Vanilla Sugar, page 108
> Vanilla Crème Brûlée: page 122

Vanilla Rice Pudding

Rice pudding is a classic, and while some people think a classic can't be bettered, amended or changed, I think the opposite. It doesn't just have to be served in huge, steaming bowls in winter – although I wouldn't complain at all if you did. I think with a light touch of vanilla and raspberries, rice pudding can be served chilled in glasses in a slightly more sophisticated way. But feel free to serve it as you please.

Makes 6 good (or 12 small) portions
Prep time 5 minutes
Cooking time 2 hours

1 litre full-fat milk
1 vanilla pod, split lengthways
50g Vanilla Sugar **>**
¼ tsp grated nutmeg
Pinch of salt
60g butter
150g arborio rice

1 Preheat the oven to 150°C/gas mark 2.

2 Put all the ingredients into an ovenproof casserole dish, stir well and pop it into the oven for 2 hours in total. After 30 minutes, open the oven door and stir it all again.

3 When it's time for the pudding to come out, it's not always set as firmly as you would like, so you must leave it to stand for a good hour. It will carry on absorbing the liquid and thicken up more.

4 Serve with raspberry or Plum Jam.

TIP
● Check the pudding after an hour and a half as oven temperatures can vary. The depth of your casserole dish may also affect the cooking time.

LINKS
> Use Lavender Sugar (page 58) instead of Vanilla Sugar and serve it chilled.
> Vanilla Sugar, page 108
> Plum Jam, page 160
> Serve piping hot made with Cardamom Sugar (page 226) and extra cardamom on a cold winter's evening, or with Orange & Clove Sugar (page 245) at Christmas.

Vanilla Crème Brûlée

It's no accident that crème brûlée appears on almost every restaurant menu. Why? Because it needs making the day before to allow the custard to set: perfect prepping. A quick sprinkle of sugar and a blast of heat and this sumptuous, voluptuous, sensuous little pot is ready to go. This lovely little number can be dressed in any flavour: vanilla, lavender, cardamom, or orange and clove. It's my little black dress of puddings.

Makes 4 x 175ml ramekins
Prep time 25 minutes
Cooking time 1 hour – but make it
1 day before it needs eating

Note: You will need 4 ramekins 5cm deep x 9cm across; they hold 175ml of custard

1 quantity Vanilla Custard **>**
80g Vanilla Sugar **>**
20ml water

1 Follow the recipe for Vanilla Custard on page 118.

2 Divide the custard into 4 ramekins and cover in cling film. Pop these in the fridge until the next day to set.

3 Make the caramel at least 1 hour before serving. Put the Vanilla Sugar and water in a heavy-based pan over a moderate heat to dissolve the sugar. Be really gentle and patient to caramelise it – you must not stir it! Simply shake and tilt the pan from side to side.

4 When all the sugar has caramelised (this takes about 10–15 minutes), you should have a clear, golden, very hot syrup. Remove from the heat and pour immediately over the custards. They should be hard within 4 minutes.

TIPS

● Save scrubbing the pan! To clean it, simply add hot water and reheat; the caramel will dissolve in the hot water, as if by magic...

● As an alternative method at step 3, simply cover the top of the crème brûlée with caster sugar and use a cook's blowtorch to caramelise it.

LINKS
> Substitute any of the following sugars for Vanilla Sugar: Lavender (page 58), Cardamom (page 226) or Orange & Clove (page 245).
> Vanilla Sugar, page 108
> Vanilla Custard, page 118

Vanilla Blondies

With all the buttery fudginess of a brownie, blondies are sweet, chewy and seriously simple to make. But it's not so easy to choose between using peanuts or pecans – so I make two versions. The pecan version is fabulous, and the salted peanut version is amazing. So why not make both?

Serves 16
Prep time 10 minutes
Cooking time 25–30 minutes

300g plain flour
2 tsp baking powder
250g unsalted butter
400g Vanilla Sugar **>**
2 eggs, beaten
225g salted peanuts or pecans
   with a pinch of sea salt

1 Preheat the oven to 175°C/gas mark 3.

2 Sift the flour and baking power into a large bowl and combine.

3 In a saucepan, melt the butter and bring it briefly to the boil and stir the sugar. It doesn't all dissolve, but the sugar goes 'gloopy'.

4 Pour the butter-sugar mixture into the flour and mix with a wooden spoon until combined. Stir in the eggs, mix well and then add the peanuts. Pour into a large 24cm x 30cm baking tray and spread.

5 Bake in the oven for 25–30 minutes, but check after 25 minutes. The tops of the blondies should be just golden brown and lightly spring back. If it needs a little longer, be careful not to overcook – blondies need to retain their fudginess. It will firm up as it cools down. Cool in the tray and cut into 16 squares when cold.

TIP
● Don't rush to cut this one into squares. It does need time to firm up.

> ### LINKS
> **>** Vanilla Sugar, page 108
> **>** Try making pecan blondies with Cardamom Sugar (page 226) or with Orange & Clove Sugar (page 245) for Christmas.

Home grown Tommy K.
Picked by L.s beans

Spiced Tomato Jam

Home
picke

wn Tommy K's

Li biana . k

Tomatoes

Red, full-flavoured, juicy tomatoes, full of sweet ripeness hanging on green herb-scented stalks... I spot tomatoes in an instant. The colour invites the eye, like a saucy lady, or a Christmas gift wrapped in a big red bow: 'Come and get me!'

Their effect in cooking gets you heading to the table in super-quick time, eager to eat. That deep, sweet, sugared tomato depth in sauces promises that the taste wrapped around the food will linger.

Spiced Tomato Jam

A burst of sweet summer tomatoes and aromatic Indian spices give this jam just the right balance of sweet intensity. I recommend a large dollop served with a hunk of Cheddar for a classic ploughman's, but it works seriously well smothered on top of a juicy beef burger for your next barbecue. You can blend your own spices, but for those of you who, like me, haven't the time, I suggest using an Indian spice blend called garam masala. It pays to be particular about this spice mix. Do not buy an own-brand version that lists dried onion or garlic powder as one of its main ingredients. It will be revolting; powdered onion has no place in garam masala. Instead, opt for a true Asian blend. Don't be tempted to drag an old pot out of the back of the cupboard, either, because it will be dull. These vibrant spices are at their best fresh from the pack.

Makes 5 x 450g jars
Prep time 30 minutes
Cooking time 20 minutes

1.5kg chopped tomatoes, skins removed
    (see 'Tips & Uses', below)
2 tbsp garam masala
1kg jam sugar
Juice and zest of 2 fresh limes
1 tbsp sea salt

TIPS & USES

● To remove tomato skins, cut a 5cm-wide cross in the bottom of each fruit, taking care not to cut into the flesh too deeply. Pop the tomatoes into a saucepan of very hot water for about 45 seconds; the skin should curl a little. Lift them out with a large spoon and transfer straight into a bowl of very cold water. Gently ease off the skins with your thumbs. If they don't ease away, return the tomatoes to the hot water and repeat.

● It really is best to keep children out of the way when you have fruit and sugar boiling at high temperatures.

● If your jam starts to spit, turn the heat down by half and stir so that the jam doesn't burn on the bottom of the pan. Bring it back up to temperature when it has calmed down.

1 Preheat the oven to 150°C/gas mark 2.

2 Put the jars (not the lids) into the oven. Put a saucer in the fridge.

3 Place the chopped tomatoes and garam masala into a pan. Cover and heat gently for about 5–7 minutes, stirring occasionally.

4 Once the consistency is liquid, add the sugar, lime juice and zest and salt, and stir.

5 Once the sugar has dissolved, bring the jam to the boil. It needs about 10–15 minutes on a good bubble.

6 As the jam boils, remove any froth that appears on the top – about half a cupful is more than enough.

7 When the jam coats the back of a metal spoon, it is ready to test. Take the pan off the heat while you do this: Pop a teaspoon of jam on the cold saucer from the fridge. After a minute, the jam should wrinkle gently when you run a spoon through the centre. If it doesn't, simply return the pan to the boil and repeat this test in another 2–3 minutes. Take care, though, not to over-boil; this setting point should really take no longer than 20 minutes to achieve, at most.

8 Take the jam jars out of the oven. While still very hot, ladle the jam into the jars using a jam funnel or jug. After a 1–2 minutes, put the lids on: the heat from the jam will ensure they're sterilised.

LINKS
> Chopped Salad, see page 131
> Chicken Puff Parcels, page 132
> Venison Burgers, page 195

Chopped Salad

This spiced salad uses Spiced Tomato Jam as a sweetener. Combined with sesame seed oil, chilli and lemon juice, it has an oriental tone to it. Feel free to add a dash of soy sauce if you want more salt. I serve this using orange in the dressing alongside Roast Pork Belly with Orange & Cloves.

6 tomatoes
Half a cucumber
2 large carrots
1 large avocado
1 little gem lettuce
1 medium-hot chilli, finely chopped
200g feta cheese
1 tbsp poppy seeds
Juice of 1 lemon (or orange)
2 tbsp Spiced Tomato Jam >
   (or ready-made mango chutney)
1 tbsp toasted sesame seed oil

1 Chop all vegetables into 2.5cm cubes. When you chop the cucumber, remember to take out the seeds in the centre before you cube it; otherwise the salad will be too wet. Pop all the chopped vegetables into a large salad bowl. Add the chilli.

2 Cut up the feta cheese into 2.5cm cubes, and add to the chopped vegetables in the bowl.

3 Throw the poppy seeds, lemon juice, jam and oil into the salad and toss really well just before serving.

TIP
● The dressing for this salad can be swapped with any of the other dressings throughout this book.

LINKS
> Spiced Tomato Jam, page 128
> Roast Pork Belly with Orange & Cloves,
   page 250

Chicken Puff Parcels

I first made these the week before my eighteenth birthday. I had a very grown-up dinner party and invited friends over for wine and canapés. They refused to believe I had made this recipe and insisted I was passing off M&S food as my own (I was rather annoyed about it all). Nowadays I get these ready up to 48 hours in advance. So if we have people coming for supper on a Friday night, all I have to do is pop them in the oven.

Serves 4
Prep time 30 minutes
Cooking time 35 minutes
Suitable for freezing Before cooking

4 tbsp olive oil
3 garlic cloves, finely sliced
1 onion, finely sliced
4 chicken breast fillets
Juice and zest of 2 oranges
4 heaped tbsp Spiced Tomato Jam >
1 tsp sea salt

1 x 375g pack of puff pastry
1 egg, beaten

TIP
● If you haven't made Spiced Tomato Jam, use mango chutney instead.

1 Preheat the oven to 170°C/gas mark 3.

2 Heat the olive oil in a pan and sauté the onion and garlic. Add the chicken breasts and cook gently, making sure they're browned on each side. Pour in the orange juice and cover the pan.

3 Turn down the heat and allow the chicken to steam in the orange juice. After about 10–12 minutes, remove the lid and check that the meat is cooked. Remove the chicken and set to one side to cool a little.

4 Add the jam and salt to the remaining sauce. Keep the heat on low and just reduce the liquid to a custard consistency. Don't turn the heat up too high; you don't want to burn the sauce. Remove from the heat and set to one side to cool.

5 Roll out the puff pastry on a well-floured surface and divide into 4 squares.

6 In the centre of each pastry square place a tablespoon of cooled sauce from the pan, then put a chicken breast on top. Draw up the four corners of the pastry and push them together to form a parcel. Turn it over and pop it straight onto a baking tray. Be sure to draw the pastry together well, as a leak will cause the sauce to run all over the tray while it's cooking. (You can freeze spare ones at this point or pop them in the fridge for up to 48 hours.)

7 Make a 2.5cm cut into the top of each parcel, then glaze the pastry with beaten egg. Pop into the oven for about 15–20 minutes until the pastry is risen and golden brown.

8 Use any remaining sauce to dress the plate and serve.

LINK
> Spiced Tomato Jam, page 128

Bolognese Sauce

I can't even begin to tell you how much I rely on this sauce. It is my mother's recipe, and I am the third generation to make it. Without it, my day-to-day culinary offering would be halved. I absolutely depend on it as the base for so many of my dishes. There are literally hundreds of variations of Bolognese, some adding carrots, onions, even celery; this one has none of those things. It is typical of my style: easy, intense and versatile. So make more. It freezes, and to be honest, it tastes so much better the following day. I almost always pair a spaghetti Bolognese with a crunchy fresh green salad and a glass of fruity Merlot.

Serves 8
Prep time 15 minutes
Cooking time 4 hours
Suitable for freezing

2 tbsp olive oil
1kg minced beef (less than 5% fat is best)
Half a garlic bulb, finely chopped
2 x 400g tins chopped tomatoes
350ml Tomato Sauce >
150g tomato purée
1 level tsp sea salt
100ml water
1 tbsp sugar (optional)
Grated Parmesan, to serve

1 In a large saucepan, heat the olive oil and add the minced beef and the garlic a little at a time. Brown the beef well; this gives the sauce extra flavour.

2 Add all the rest of the ingredients (apart from the Parmesan), mix well and bring almost to the boil.

3 Reduce the heat and simmer on a very low heat for 4 hours. Check regularly that the sauce is not sticking to the base of the pan; stir and add a drop of water if it looks too gloopy.

4 After 4 hours, the sauce should be a dark, rich, deep-red colour and have an intense sweet-tomato flavour. Taste. Adjust the seasoning if necessary by adding a little more salt, and a tablespoon of sugar if you like it slightly sweeter.

5 Serve with spaghetti and plenty of fresh Parmesan.

LINKS
> Stuffed Tomatoes, page 136
> Tomato Sauce, page 139
> Neapolitan Casa Pie, page 145
> Check out the pasty recipe on page 191 and use the sauce with the mash for fabulous pasties!

Stuffed Tomatoes

For a quick-turnaround lunch, these stuffed tomatoes make a super summer dish. I know you'll think eating two of these is greedy, but although they look large, they're mainly tomato and not as filling as you think. In any case, they're delicious, so think 'seconds'. You'll be glad you made more.

Serves 4
Prep time 10 minutes
Setting time 25 minutes

8 large beef tomatoes
250g cooked rice
550g Bolognese Sauce **>**
100g grated Parmesan
Basil, black pepper and salad to garnish

TIP
● Use as a starter or a summer barbecue dish.

1 Preheat the oven to 175°C/gas mark 4. Slice 2cm off the top of the tomatoes and keep to one side as the tops to put back on. Scoop out the flesh from inside the tomatoes, making sure you don't cut too far in. Place the tomatoes on a baking tray.

2 Mix together the rice, sauce and half the Parmesan. Fill the tomatoes with this mixture and sprinkle with the remaining Parmesan and a grind or two of pepper before putting their tops back on. Transfer to the oven for 20 minutes.

3 Serve on a bed of green salad.

LINK
> Bolognese Sauce, page 135

Tomato Sauce

This recipe is a base – a foundation, if you will, packed to the very core with flavours that will give you some seriously delicious food options. It's so sweet, deep and fragrant with garden herbs, I really advise you to double this if you can and make as much as your pan will hold.

Makes 1.5 litres of sauce
Prep time 20 minutes
Cooking time 4 hours 20 minutes
Suitable for freezing

4 tbsp olive oil
1 onion, roughly chopped
4 sticks of celery, roughly chopped
2kg tomatoes, quartered,
    or 2 litres tinned tomatoes
5 garlic cloves
2 large carrots, roughly chopped
Handful of fresh basil
Black pepper

1 Heat the olive oil in a large 3-4 litre heavy-based pan and sauté the onion.

2 Add all the other ingredients, cover and reduce the temperature of the hob to a lowish setting, allowing the tomatoes to cook in their own steam for about 20 minutes.

3 When you remove the lid, the tomatoes should be squishy and you'll need to give the sauce a good stir. Leave the pan on the hob for about 3–4 hours on low, just bubbling away.

4 Remove the pan from the hob. Once cool enough to handle, pour the mixture through a sieve, pressing every last drop through with the back of a wooden spoon. Discard any remaining contents in the sieve.

5 Store in an airtight container in the fridge for up to 5 days.

TIPS & USES
● Use this sauce to make tomato soup. Take 1 litre and simmer on the hob for about 30 minutes. Stir in 200ml single cream and some black pepper and serve. It's that easy!

● Tinned tomatoes give a much deeper colour to tomato sauce than fresh.

LINKS
> Bolognese Sauce, page 135
> Meatballs in Tomato Sauce, page 140
> Easy Pasta Bake, page 149
> Serve as Tomato Soup with Caraway
   & Parmesan Muffins, page 183.

Meatballs in Tomato Sauce

I can't eat meatballs without smiling. My brother at age six was the most pernickety eater imaginable. Once in France he really took to a dish of meatballs in the local restaurant. My mother was literally crying with laughter as he asked for a third helping. I asked what was so funny and she just about managed to say that they were testicles. Aged seven, I was still none the wiser – but these meatballs are just as tender, juicy and delicious.

Serves 4
Prep time 15 minutes
Cooking time 35 minutes
Suitable for freezing At step 2

500g minced beef
A handful finely chopped fresh herbs,
    such as dill, parsley, coriander
80g breadcrumbs
½ tsp paprika
2 dashes Worcestershire sauce
Pinch of salt
2 finely minced garlic cloves
1 litre Tomato Sauce **>**
    or shop-bought passata
3 tbsp rapeseed oil
30g toasted almond slices, to garnish

TIP
● To get ahead in the kitchen, make double and freeze half. I know it's obvious, but sometimes we need reminding of the little things that get us ahead.

1 Preheat the oven to 180°C/gas mark 4.

2 Mix all the ingredients, except the Tomato Sauce, oil and almonds, in a bowl until well-blended. Form into golf-ball-size balls. (At this point I pop some of mine in a tin and put them away in the freezer).

3 Heat the oil in a heavy, high-sided pan suitable for the oven and sauté the meatballs gently for 5 minutes. Don't move them around too much; they'll break apart if you're too heavy-handed.

4 After 5 minutes, they should be sealed on the outside. Pour in the tomato sauce and put in the oven for 30 minutes. Serve on a bed of rice and scatter with herbs and toasted almonds.

LINK
> Tomato Sauce, page 139

Neapolitan Casa Pie

This glam-sounding pie is actually a result of my sense of the ridiculous. It is just a cottage pie made with Bolognese Sauce, but the ostentatious title tickled me no end! It is seriously delicious and simple, takes minutes to assemble and is hugely welcome at the end of a busy day just to pop in the oven and serve with a salad.

Serves 6
Prep time 10 minutes
Cooking time 35–40 minutes
Suitable for freezing Be sure to defrost before reheating.

1kg Bolognese Sauce >
1kg new potatoes, cooked
8–10 whole black peppercorns, crushed
Pinch of sea salt
Fresh oregano, to garnish

1 Preheat the oven to 180°C/gas mark 4.

2 Put the Bolognese Sauce in a large baking dish. Using the palm of your hand, slightly squash the potatoes and arrange across the top of the pie.

3 Scatter with cracked black pepper and salt. At this point you could put it either in the fridge for up to 2 days or the freezer for up to 3 months.

4 Bake in the oven for 35–40 minutes.

TIP
● Make mini pies without the salt in ramekins and freeze them for a children's supper. They cook from frozen at the same temperature, so pop them in the oven as you go out on the school run and 25–30 minutes later they'll be ready as you walk back in the house. Very useful indeed.

LINKS
> Bolognese Sauce, page 135
> Any potato left over from making Caraway & Lemon Potato Cakes (page 188) makes a cracking good topping for this pie, too.

Tomato & Garlic Pasta

The exact origins of this recipe are lost in the mists of time, but my mother is Italian, so there's a connection with Naples somewhere. I've called it Tomato & Garlic Pasta, but since I was a child, it has always been known as 'Garlic Yum Yum'. Despite the huge amount of garlic, it's the intense, sweet tomato that comes to the front of the palate, with a soft, mellow garlic base under the rich sauce. The speed with which you can take the ingredients out of the cupboard and have this on the table is impressive. By the time the pasta has boiled, it should be about ready. Whenever my husband has a meeting with a particularly pretty client the following day, you can be certain we will have this deliciously simple dish for supper. Trust me and try it out. It works!

Makes 4
Prep time 10 minutes
Cooking time 10–12 minutes

1 whole medium garlic bulb
500g spaghetti
1 x 200g tube tomato purée
80ml extra-virgin olive oil
120g fresh Parmesan, grated, for serving

1 Peel and finely chop all the garlic cloves. Put the pasta on to cook according to the instructions on the packet. I allow 80–100g per person of dry spaghetti. Add a teaspoon of salt and a dash of olive oil to the water before cooking.

2 Heat the olive oil in a saucepan for 1–2 minutes. Test it's hot enough by dropping a small piece of garlic in: when it sizzles, the pan is ready, so add the rest of the garlic and sauté for about 1–2 minutes. You're not looking to brown the garlic at all, so you must keep the heat at a medium temperature.

3 Stir in the tomato purée and turn the heat down to a slightly lower temperature. Keep stirring. As the tomato cooks, it incorporates most of the oil and turns from a fresh red to a deeper, darker red. After 5–7 minutes it should be done.

4 Drain your pasta and add it to the tomato sauce, stirring well. Serve immediately with freshly grated Parmesan.

LINK
> Use the sauce as the base for Tomato Pizza, page 150.

Easy Pasta Bake

This is the sort of meal to have ready when you get in from a long walk, or for supper after the theatre. I couldn't live without it, and it's so easy and delicious. The Parmesan and pancetta give it a sophisticated balance. The flavour of the homemade Tomato Sauce is so authentically Italian that you can imagine eating it in the square in Sienna.

Serves 8
Prep time 20 minutes
Cooking time 30 minutes
Suitable for freezing

1.5kg Tomato Sauce **>** (or bought passata)
1 x 500g packet dried pennoni (larger
 version of penne) or cannelloni
Handful of basil leaves

For the filling
150g pancetta slices, chopped
4 bread slices, blitzed to crumbs
 in a food processor
1 tsp nutmeg
6 tbsp chopped fresh oregano
Grated zest and juice of 2 lemons
200g Gruyère, Taleggio or Ogle Shield★
4 large egg yolks

★ *Ogle Shield is a British washed-rind cheese
 which I think is absolutely divine.*

For the topping
4 slices of bread blitzed
 into breadcrumbs
6 tbsp grated Parmesan
½ teaspoon sweet smoked paprika

1 Preheat the oven to 200°C/gas mark 6.

2 Put the Tomato Sauce in a saucepan, season to taste, bring to the boil, cover and simmer gently for 5 minutes. If using commercial Tomato Sauce instead of the homemade sauce, then add 2 garlic cloves, a glass of red wine, a tablespoon of sugar and a good handful of basil leaves finely chopped, and simmer this for 20 minutes before proceeding with step 3.

3 Cut the pancetta into small pieces; dry-fry in a pan. Reserve a handful to scatter on the cooked pasta.

4 In a large pan of boiling water, cook the pasta for 5 minutes, then drain and refresh in cold water. Meanwhile, mix the breadcrumbs, nutmeg, pancetta, oregano, zest and juice, cheese and egg yolks and combine well. Push some of the filling into each of the pasta tubes.

5 Pour about half of the Tomato Sauce into a large ovenproof dish. Put the pasta on top and then pour over the remaining sauce. Scatter with the Parmesan and the breadcrumb and paprika mix and bake for 25 minutes. Cover with foil if browning too much. Sprinkle with chopped oregano before serving.

6 Serve with a big fresh, green salad and a fruity, fun-loving Italian wine.

LINK
> Tomato Sauce, page 139

TIP
● This dish is quicker to make using cannelloni. Pennoni, while delicious, takes more time to fill.

Double Cook: Tomato Pizza & Oregano Bread

Two for one: fresh baked bread and homemade pizza. Fast food just doesn't get much better than this. Pizza is easy and fun to make and kids love to get involved. Spelt flour makes it satisfying and it has a nutty texture that is lightened by the yeast. The addition of the fragrant oregano gives both the bread and the pizza real Mediterranean depth. Honey-sweetened tomato has an intensified flavour, the result of reducing it slowly. It's delicious, and worth taking the time to make the dough. Add good-quality mature Cheddar and this pizza has depth and natural saltiness. What I really love about this recipe, though, is that, for absolutely no extra effort, I can bake a loaf of bread at the same time. There are no extra ingredients or clearing up and it takes no time to make it. In my world, that's smart cooking!

Makes 2 x 23cm pizzas &
   1 loaf of bread
Prep time 2 hours 20 minutes
Cooking time 10 minutes for the pizzas; 25 minutes for the bread
Suitable for freezing

For the dough
3 tsp sugar
12g dried yeast
Lukewarm water
3 tsp rapeseed oil
2 tbsp dried oregano
3 tsp salt
225g wholemeal spelt flour
450g plain spelt four

For the pizza sauce
600ml Tomato Sauce **>**
   or 600g tinned chopped tomatoes
2 level tsp oregano
1 tbsp runny honey
100g grated strong mature Cheddar

LINKS
> Tomato Sauce: page 139
> Use the sauce from Tomato & Garlic Pasta (page 146) instead of plain Tomato Sauce, but be warned: you don't need much – it's intense! About 3–4 tbsp spread thinly should be enough!

---

1 Put the sugar and yeast into a bowl or jug and add 200ml of lukewarm water; too hot and it will kill the yeast, too cold and it won't activate. Allow this to sit for 10 minutes somewhere warm.

2 Add the oil. Put all the dried ingredients into a large bowl and make a well in the centre. Add the yeast to the dry mix. Using a little more water at a time, mix into dough. The amount of water varies according to the flour so I haven't given quantities. But it is best that the dough isn't too dry or it won't pick up all the flour. Add the water slowly, though; it shouldn't be too wet, either.

3 Knead on a floured surface for 10 minutes by hand or in a food processor. Set this aside somewhere warm and cover with a clean damp tea towel for 2 hours.

4 In a heavy-based saucepan add the sauce or tinned tomato, oregano and honey. Bring to the boil, then turn down to a very low heat. Simmer gently, stirring occasionally, for about 45 minutes until the tomatoes are reduced at least by half. Set aside to cool.

5 Put the dough onto a floured surface and knead gently. You can freeze it at this point. Cut a third of the dough away.

6 Cut the third into 2 pieces and roll both into 23cm squares. Transfer to baking trays and share the tomato base equally between the two, ensuring that it's evenly distributed. Scatter the cheese over the top.

7 Preheat the oven to 230°C/gas mark 8 and bake for about 8–10 minutes. Allow to cool a little before serving as this improves both the texture and flavour.

8 Transfer the remaining two-thirds of the dough into a lightly oiled bread tin. Drop the temperature of the oven (leave the oven door open for a minute or two) to 180°C/gas mark 4 and bake for 20–25 minutes. You can test when the bread is cooked by tapping the base. It should sound hollow, but if it doesn't, return it to the tin and bake for another 5 minutes. Transfer to a wire rack and allow to cool.

TIPS & USES

● If you can't find spelt flour, use ordinary wholemeal plain flour (NOT bread flour).

● If you can bear to leave it, this pizza is superb cold.

● Dough, bread and sauce freeze well, so on Friday nights I'm prepped at the end of a long day for an easy, economical start to the weekend.

● Serve the pizza with laughter and ice cream and enjoy your bread with a hunk of cheese for tomorrow's lunch.

Plum

*Plums in all their forms
are like jewels tumbling
from trees at the end of
the summer. Mirabelles,
greengages, Victorias…
their smooth, tight skins
wrap evocatively
around tart, sweet,
soft flesh. To me, they
are the most erotic fruit.
I feel the need to touch
them, caress them, and
gather them into the
basket to return with
me to my kitchen, where
they will be roasted,
stewed and baked
with all manner of
delicious ingredients.*

*I have a thing about
plums. That's why
there is a whole
chapter dedicated
to them. As autumn
sets in across
Northamptonshire,
where I live, the last
of the county's plums
can be found in the
local farm shops.*

Plum Brandy

The deep, sweet plumminess of the fruit infuses into the brandy, leaving a sweetened liquor with a dark-pink hue: autumn in a glass. By the time the plums are dropping off the trees in the last warmth of summer, I'm planning for Christmas. This plum brandy is so versatile. It makes a unique gift and forms the base for a superb cocktail. I also use it in my mincemeat sometimes, in place of Orange & Clove Brandy. (Shhhh: I always enjoy a tipple while I'm stirring the pan!)

Makes about 1.3 litres
Prep time 10 minutes

1kg plums
750g sugar
1 litre brandy

1 Wash and dry the plums, prick them with a skewer (a cocktail stick will break), then pop them into a 2-litre kilner-type jar, with a lid that seals.

2 Pour in the brandy, then add the sugar. Gently shake the jar and put it somewhere visible.

3 For the next week or so, shake the jar each day until the sugar is dissolved, then hide it away in a cupboard for at least 2 months.

LINKS
> Tipover Trifle, page 52
> Plum Brandy Cocktail, page 159
> Instant Cranberry & Brandy
  Mincemeat, page 253

TIP
● I generally decant mine after 6–8 months; if you leave it for longer, the plums can sometimes break down and you get bits floating in the brandy. If that happens, don't panic: simply use a clean piece of muslin to filter these out. They're not harmful, just not pretty!

Plum Brandy Cocktail

When my sister and her husband visit, I'm reminded of my pre-children days. The time spent on hair, make-up and wearing fabulous heels! Of course, they're not up at the crack of dawn with little ones needing breakfast, so out come the cocktail glasses and I can't resist feeling sexy and grown-up with one of these. I can't claim this mix as my own – it belongs to my brother-in-law, James. But I can say that it should always be drunk with a large bowl of olives, great conversation, laughter and wearing a pair of killer heels!

For each cocktail, you will need:
1 part Plum Brandy **>**
1½ parts gin
1 part fresh lemon juice

(1 part = 25ml)

To serve
40g salt (I use Himalayan pink salt)
A wedge of lemon

1 First, prepare your cocktail glass. Pop the salt into a saucer, use the lemon wedge to rub a generous amount of juice around the rim of the glass, then dip it into the salt and agitate to cover as much as you want.

2 Fill your cocktail shaker with ice and add the brandy, gin and lemon juice. Shake vigorously (with a little hip wiggle) and pour immediately into your frosted glass. Serve immediately.

LINK
> Plum Brandy, page 156

TIP
● Try making this with lime instead of lemon juice.

Plum Jam

There are all types of plums, including Victoria plums and greengages, and any will do for this recipe. You can find locally grown ones in farm shops, but explore a little further in the countryside and you may be lucky and discover a mirabelle or damson tree. Check with the owners first, but generally people would prefer to see fruit made into jam rather than get eaten by wasps. These sleek, round, shiny fruits really do make the most scrumptious jam. And what could be better than a cup of hot tea and plum jam over hot buttered toast in the morning?

Makes 6–7 x 450g jars
Prep time 1 hour
Cooking time 15 minutes

2kg plums (washed, stones removed)
1.5kg jam sugar

1 Heat the oven to 150°C/ gas mark 2. Pop a small plate or saucer into the fridge. Put the jars (not the lids) on a baking tray and put them in the oven.

2 Chop the plums and put them in a large pan over a low heat. Cover and stir occasionally for about 8 minutes. Once the fruit is soft, add the sugar and stir until it dissolves.

3 The jam needs 10–15 minutes on a rolling bubble. Stir occasionally. As it boils, scoop off any froth (it looks rather like soapsuds) to improve its clarity. There should be no more than half a cup of froth.

4 When the jam coats the back of a metal spoon, it's ready to test for setting point. The best test I know is the wrinkle test. Remove the saucepan from the heat while you test. Put a blob of jam the size of a ten-pence piece on the cold saucer from the fridge. After a minute or so the jam should be cool and wrinkle a little as you run your finger through the centre. If not, simply return the saucepan to the boil and repeat this test in another 2–3 minutes.

5 Remove the jars from the oven. Ladle the hot jam into the hot jars using a jam funnel or small jug. Put the lids on after 1 minute; the heat from the jam will ensure the lids are sterilised. Be careful not to burn yourself and don't worry if a jar lid isn't done up tightly. You can tighten it once the jars have cooled.

LINKS
> Use instead of Rhubarb Jam in Tipover Trifle: page 52.
> Serve with Vanilla Rice Pudding: page 121.
> Roast Duck Breast with Noodles & Chinese Duck Canapés, page 167
> Victoria Sandwich Cake, page 176

TIP
● Use the plum's delicious cousins, nectarines and peaches, to make a superb jam by following the same recipe.

Spicy
Plum
Chutney
a gift

Plum Chutney

I owe my chutney-making skills to my mother. The warm, spiced, sweet vinegary smell greets me often as I walk into the farmhouse where there is a pot on the aga almost daily in the autumn. She uses chutney and her fabulous smile as currency with almost anyone she has dealings with. So it's rare to see a plumber, chimney sweep or carpet cleaner leave without a pot of something delicious. This deeply plumy, sweet chutney is a store-cupboard staple and pretty much guarantees a fast, efficient appointment the next time your boiler breaks. It is outstanding with mellow mature Cheddar or as an accompaniment to a curry.

Makes 10 x 450g jars
Prep time 1 hour
Cooking time 4 hours
Stores 12 months

Vegetable oil, for frying
1 red onion, finely chopped
2 tsp mixed spice
1 tsp ground cloves
1 tsp ground cardamom
6 star anise
2 large Bramley apples, diced
300g mixed dried fruit
600g soft brown sugar
500ml Vanilla Vinegar **>**
4kg plums, halved and stoned

1 Heat the oil in a large saucepan and gently sauté the chopped onions until they have softened, then add the spices and cook for another minute. Stir well.

2 Add in the diced apple and dried fruit to the pan and stir it all together. Then put the sugar and vinegar into the pan and stir the mixture until it is well-combined. Add the plums.

3 Bring the chutney to the boil, then simmer for 3–4 hours on a very low heat, stirring occasionally, until the mixture has reduced – it should be thick and glossy. It won't be as thick as chutney until it cools and sets, but the consistency at this point should be like at thick tomato ketchup.

4 Spoon the chutney into sterilised jars and seal with vinegar-proof lids or a waxed paper circle and cellophane.

TIPS & USES
● This chutney is best kept in a cool, dark place for at least 1 month, but it really is better if you can bear to leave it for 3 months!

● If you don't have any Vanilla Vinegar to hand, simply add a vanilla pod, split it lengthways and use white-wine vinegar instead.

> **LINK**
> **>** Vanilla Vinegar, page 109

Plum, Mint & Couscous Salad

This is super-quick to make, and if there's a time I feel one ought be outside enjoying the last of the summer, it's when the plums come out. It's not that I don't want to cook; I just don't want to be inside on the last autumn days – I resent missing the last rays of summer. This semi-hot salad can be made in minutes, uses plums in a savoury way and means we can eat a super lunch and get straight back out into the garden. There is also very little washing up! If you want to give it a bit more substance, then a good crumbly feta or strips of Parmesan go well with it, too.

Serves 4
Prep time 15 minutes
Setting time 10 minutes

6 ripe plums, quartered
Olive oil, for brushing
½ tsp sea salt
Black pepper
750g cooked couscous
30g butter
Vanilla Vinegar **>**
 (or plain, if preferred)
Juice of 1 lemon
6 tbsp olive oil
1 tsp Dijon mustard
Toasted pine nuts
Fresh mint leaves, to dress

1 Preheat the oven to 180°C/gas mark 4.

2 Put the plums in a baking dish, brush them with a little olive oil, sprinkle with some sea salt and black pepper and roast in the oven for about 10 minutes. They still need to retain some bite.

3 In the meantime, prepare about 750g of couscous (cooked weight) according to the instructions on the packet. As you add the hot water, stir in the butter with a fork.

4 Mix together the Vanilla Vinegar, lemon juice, olive oil and Dijon mustard. Mix well and fluff through the couscous.

5 Add the baked plums, scatter with toasted pine nuts and serve dressed with mint leaves.

TIPS & USES
● Roast the plums in the baking dish you are going to serve it in. This saves washing up and it's pre-warmed to keep that salad hot at the table.

● Use as a packed lunch.

● Terrific as an 'instant picnic' instead of sandwiches.

LINKS
> Use Elderflower & Lime Salad Dressing (page 18) or Lemon Salad Dressing (page 98).
> Vanilla Vinegar, page 109

Double Cook: Roast Duck Breast with Noodles & Chinese Duck Canapés

Just thinking about preparing canapés before guests arrive can send me into a panic. Between clearing the devastation the children have created and making sure the drinks are chilled and the meal itself is on track, I have no time to faff around with dainty little morsels. This leaves me with two options: buy some or prep for some. This way you get a simple supper that gives you the opportunity to put some canapés in the freezer (or you can make them up to three days in advance). In case you forget, the whole point of inviting people over is to enjoy yourself – and being one step ahead means you can do just that!

Roast Duck Breast with Noodles

Makes 2 main dishes plus 24 canapés
Prep time 20 plus 10 minutes
Cooking time for both 25 minutes
plus 12 minutes
Suitable for freezing Only the canapés

For the noodles
4 duck breasts
Toasted sesame seed oil
3 plums, stones removed,
   sliced in 4 pieces
½ tsp Chinese five spice
Pinch of salt
4 tbsp Plum Brandy **>**
3 tbsp dark soy sauce
2–3 nests of egg noodles
Fresh mint
2–3 shallots
2 garlic cloves
1 chilli, finely chopped

For the canapés
2 of the cooked duck breasts left over
   from the recipe above
2–3 shallots, finely chopped
2 garlic cloves, finely chopped
3 tbsp Plum Jam **>**
4 sheets filo pastry (not frozen)
20g melted butter
35g feta cheese
Fresh mint to garnish

1 Preheat the oven to 200°C/gas mark 6.

2 Make 4 x 5cm cuts across each duck breast. This allows the fat to escape and gives you a nice, crispy skin. Brush a very small amount of the sesame seed oil into a pan that can be transferred to the oven and place each duck breast skin-side down. Add the plums. Add the Chinese five spice and a pinch of salt, sprinkling evenly over the duck. Allow the duck to sizzle away on the hob for a good 8–10 minutes.

3 Once the duck breasts are golden and crispy on both sides, transfer to the oven for 20 minutes. Leave the plums in the pan. Remove the duck from the oven and return the pan to the hob. Add the brandy and soy sauce to the pan, stir a little and return to the oven for a further 5–8 minutes.

4 In the meantime, prepare the noodles according to the instructions on the packet.

5 Take the duck breasts from the oven. Leave 2 in the pan for the canapés. Take 2 breasts and slice them into 0.5cm strips. Use 4–5 tablespoons of the juices from the pan and toss with the noodles, coating them well. Serve immediately with the duck on top, and scatter with fresh mint and finely chopped chillies.

Chinese Duck Canapés

TIPS & USES

● To check the meat is cooked, a meat thermometer should read over 72°C. But as long as the duck breasts have had 20 minutes at the right temperature they should be fine.

● If you don't like duck or can't find any, then good lamb steaks are a great substitute. Follow the recipe as before, but note that at Step 3, lamb steaks take just 3 minutes.

LINKS
> If you don't have Plum Brandy, use a good quality balsamic vinegar or Vanilla Vinegar (page 109) instead.
> Plum Brandy page 156
> Plum Jam, page 160

1 When the remaining two duck breasts have cooled enough to handle, slice them into small (1cm) pieces. Sauté the shallots and garlic in the original pan (there should be enough oil left over). Once they are lightly browned, add the meat to the pan along with the Plum Jam. Stir well.

2 Prepare the filo pastry by layering 4 pieces together, brushing a layer of melted butter between each sheet as you do so. Cut into 16 squares about 6cm across. Pop these into a mini muffin tray, fill with a tablespoon of the duck mixture and scatter bits of feta over them. At this point I cover them with cling film and put them away in the tray in either the fridge or the freezer.

3 When you're ready to cook them, they need just 12 minutes in the oven at 175°C/gas mark 3. Once cooked, allow them to cool for a few minutes before putting them onto a plate and scattering with fresh mint leaves.

Plum & Cardamom Crumble

Crumble may be a bit old-fashioned, but adding a layer of cardamom and jazzing up the topping brings a fresh perspective to this classic dish. The time to make it is at the end of August, when the evenings just start to draw in. Deep, dark plums sit stewed in sweetness under a light, aromatic, crunchy topping. For me, it has to be served in a great puddle of creamy Vanilla Custard. The cardamom binds with the rich, plummy base; the vanilla in the custard floats effortlessly across the top, and there you have it: a sophisticated crumble.

Serves 6–8
Prep time 15 minutes
Cooking time 35–40 minutes
Suitable for freezing

For the base
800g plums, stoned and halved
60g sugar
25g butter

For the topping
230g rolled oats
125g sweetened desiccated coconut
100g flaked almonds
50g sugar
1 level tsp ground cardamom
150ml rapeseed oil

1 Preheat the oven to 180°C/gas mark 4.

2 Put the plums in an ovenproof dish about 25cm wide and 5cm deep. Sprinkle the sugar and butter over them evenly.

3 Mix all the dry ingredients together, then drizzle the rapeseed oil over the top. Mix really well.

4 Sprinkle the topping over the plums and bake in the oven for 35 minutes, until the topping is a light golden brown and the fruit is bubbling away underneath.

5 Wait a few minutes for the crumble to cool before serving with warm Vanilla Custard or thick cream.

TIP
● Make double the topping and you'll have a large pot of granola for breakfast. Just put the crumble to bake on the top oven shelf while you put the rest of the topping onto a baking tray and bake it on the bottom shelf, turning once or twice to check it.

> **LINK**
> Vanilla Custard, page 118

Plum Cobbler

If I'm making scones, then I make a cobbler. If I make a cobbler, then I make scones. It's the same ingredients, the same clearing up, so for the same effort I can take a batch of freshly baked scones to a friend's for afternoon tea and have a cobbler ready and waiting for supper. Simple, effective delicious and time-saving: just double the Scones recipe on page 175.

Serves 6–8
Prep time 20 minutes
Cooking time 25 minutes

750g plums, stoned and halved
40g unsalted butter
100g Cardamom Sugar **>**
Zest and juice of 1 orange
½ tsp allspice
30g soft brown sugar
125g mascarpone

For the topping
Scone mix **>**
1 egg, beaten, for brushing

1 Preheat the oven to 190°C/gas mark 5. Put the plums, butter, sugar and orange zest and juice into an ovenproof dish 26cm across and about 6cm deep.

2 Mix the scone base (follow instructions on page 175) and cut out any shape you like in small scones, such as hearts, rounds or stars.

3 Mix the allspice and the brown sugar into the mascarpone and dollop it on top of the plums.

4 Arrange the cut-out scones on top and lay them as close together as possible. Don't worry if you can still see little bits of plum through the shapes; the scone mix will rise and expand. Brush the scones with the beaten egg.

5 Pop the dish into the oven for 25 minutes, or until the scones (now dumplings) are golden brown. Cool for 5–6 minutes and serve.

TIP
● Make this cobbler with virtually any combination of fruit and flavours to suit; just substitute other flavoured sugars for the Cardamom Sugar. Try Gooseberry & Vanilla, Apple made with Orange & Clove Sugar at Christmas, or Rhubarb & Cardamom Sugar in spring.

LINKS
> Vanilla Sugar, page 108
> Scones, page 175
> Cardamom Sugar, page 226
> Orange & Clove Sugar, page 245

Scones

I use this recipe as the topping for Plum Cobbler, but you can make it on its own. It doubles easily to make more and you can swap flavours at a moment's notice. Lavender scones are superb served with strawberry jam; warm orange and clove scones smothered in brandy butter are great to give to carol singers at Christmas, or try cardamom scones served in the afternoon with Plum Jam and a pot of Earl Grey tea.

Makes 8
Prep time 5 minutes
Cooking time 20 minutes
Suitable for freezing

225g self-raising flour
75g slightly salted butter, chilled,
   cut in small pieces
¼ tsp salt
50g Vanilla Sugar **>**
125ml buttermilk
   (ordinary milk will do)
3–4 tbsp milk
Extra flour, for dusting
Vanilla Sugar **>**
   for sprinkling
1 egg, beaten, for the glaze

1 Preheat the oven to 180°C/gas mark 4.

2 Put the flour, butter, salt and sugar into a bowl. Mix well. Make a well in the centre and add the buttermilk. Bring the mixture together to form a dough. If the dough seems a bit too dry, add a little more buttermilk, a teaspoon at a time.

3 Turn out onto a floured work surface and use your hands to form a 2.5cm round. Cut out shapes from this, depending on your preference, and put them on a baking tray.

4 Glaze the scones with the beaten egg and bake for 18–20 minutes. Sprinkle with Vanilla Sugar.

5 Cool on a wire rack. If you want to freeze these scones, do so as soon as they are cool. They are best enjoyed on the same day.

LINKS
> Vanilla Sugar, page 108
> Plum Cobbler, page 172

Victoria Sandwich Cake

If I were to choose a different name I would choose Victoria. It's elegant, classic and has the queen of cakes as a namesake. With no ego at all, I wonder if this version should be known as a Vanessa Sandwich Cake? The twist here is replacing the usual vanilla with cardamom. The sweet, deep plum jam is met with spiced cardamom, combining like lovers dancing cheek to cheek. It's a classic. My only real piece of advice is to make two. That way you can freeze one and not begrudge anyone having a rather larger-than-polite slice!

Serves 8–10
Prep time 15 minutes
Cooking time 25 minutes
Suitable for freezing Before filling and decorating

For the cake
250g butter or margarine
 (suitable for baking)
250g Cardamom Sugar **>**
250g self-raising flour
4 large eggs

For the filling
175g Plum Jam **>**
325ml double cream
1 tbsp icing sugar, for dusting

1 Preheat the oven to 180°C/gas mark 4.

2 Using a hand mixer or food mixer, cream together the butter or margarine and Cardamom Sugar. Beat well until white and fluffy.

3 Add 3–4 tablespoons of flour to the mixture, then add the eggs. Adding the flour like this prevents the mixture from curdling. (If it does, just keep adding flour a little at a time, beating the mixture to ensure it is evenly distributed.) Add in the rest of the flour gradually and mix well.

4 Divide the mixture between 23cm round cake tins and bake in the oven for 20–25 minutes, until firm to the touch. Cool on a wire rack.

5 Once the cakes are cool, spoon jam onto one half. Whip the cream until it is thick but not overly stodgy. Spoon this carefully onto the jam and sandwich the layers of cake together.

6 Finish it off with a light dusting of icing sugar.

LINKS
> The base here is the same recipe for Vanilla & Rhubarb Cupcakes (page 33), although it uses Cardamom instead of Vanilla Sugar.
> Plum Jam, page 160
> Cardamom Sugar, page 226

Caraway

These small, beautifully formed, crescent-shaped seeds really have irresistible charm. Even the name caraway reflects just how this spice carries me away. In an instant I am in the Middle East, eating spiced rice on a Turkish carpet.

Caraway lifts and romanticises all sorts of dishes. Just a hint of it wafting across the kitchen promises deliciousness to come. Its exotic, mellow, deep fragrance blends into our western cooking, adding drama and mystery to the everyday.

Caraway Crackers

The recipe that inspired these is by Yotam Ottolenghi. He is one of my all-time food heroes, blending flavours like no one else I know. The caraway is my own twist, and these certainly make an impression. Wonderfully theatrical, they create a showy centrepiece: the seeds are especially pretty in candlelight as the crackers take on a translucent quality. I stack them in a tall jug or vase to serve with a large cheese platter and figs at a dinner party. They also have a satisfying crunch, with an overlay of sweet caraway and warmth from the paprika. They go particularly well with a softer cheese. A good, round-bellied port doesn't go amiss, either.

Makes about 30
Prep time 15 minutes, plus 1 hour
for chilling
Cooking time 6 minutes
Suitable for freezing Prior to baking

300g plain flour
½ tsp cream of tartar
1 tsp baking powder
1 tsp paprika
½ tsp garam masala
1 heaped tbsp caraway seeds
135ml ice-cold water
50ml olive oil mixed with 20ml toasted
    sesame seed oil
Sea salt to season

1 Put all the dry ingredients into a mixing bowl and stir to mix in the spices evenly.

2 Add the water and mix to form into a dough. Form into a sausage shape, cover this in cling film and pop it into the fridge to chill for about an hour.

3 Heat the oven to 220°C/gas mark 7. On a lightly floured surface cut off chunks about the size of a ping-pong ball and roll each out as thinly as possible. Try to keep the shape long and thin; they look elegant this way.

4 Brush both sides with the oil, sprinkle with a little sea salt and bake for 6 minutes.

LINK
> For a lemony taste, use 110ml ice-cold water mixed with 25ml Lemon Syrup (page 82) instead of plain water.

Caraway & Parmesan Muffins

More often than not, when I've been in the garden for the day the very last thing I want to do is cook a meal. My get-out is a ploughman's: a large hunk of cheese with a pot of Spiced Tomato Jam or Plum Chutney together with some crispy salad and these hot, buttered Caraway and Parmesan Muffins. It's easy food. They also make absolutely fabulous accompaniments to pretty much any soup.

Makes 8 muffins
Prep time 10 minutes
Cooking time 20–25 minutes
Suitable for freezing

280g plain flour
155g Parmesan, grated
1 tbsp baking powder
2 tbsp Cardamom Sugar **>**
1 tsp caraway seeds
1 large egg
4 tbsp rapeseed oil
250ml milk

1 Preheat the oven to 190°C/gas mark 5. Grease a muffin tin.

2 In a large bowl mix together the flour, Parmesan, baking powder, sugar and caraway seeds.

3 In a large jug, whisk the egg, oil and milk until blended. Make a well in the centre of the dry mix and pour in the liquid. Stir well for about 1 minute but no more, even if the batter is still a little lumpy.

4 Fill the muffin cups almost full and bake for 20–25 minutes until they are golden and springy to the touch. Allow the muffins to cool for about 5 minutes, then transfer them to a wire rack.

TIP
● Replace the caraway with a teaspoon of dried lavender for lavender muffins.

> **LINKS**
> **>** Serve with Tomato Soup, page 139
> **>** Cardamom Sugar, page 226

Double Cook: Caraway & Lemon Pumpkin Soup and Pumpkin Pie

Pumpkins are magnificent, playing a major part in the autumn food stash. Initially, I'm intimidated by them: they look burly and tough and are often large. In reality, pumpkins are actually soft and buttery once cooked, but I have to remind myself of that. They make super soup, fabulous pies and are great just roasted and tossed in herbs and butter, so they're well worth tackling. Exposed to a constant gentle dry heat that softens and sweetens them, the fruit develops a depth of flavour that becomes the base for a mellow soup or pie. Deep-orange, with citrus-fruit overtones and caraway undertones, this is a sweet autumnal taste.

Caraway & Lemon Pumpkin Soup

Serves 8
Prep time 12 minutes,
plus 1 hour roasting
Cooking time 10 minutes
Suitable for freezing

1.8kg pumpkin
2 tbsp olive oil
Pinch of salt
Zest of 2 unwaxed lemons
2 level tbsp caraway seeds
100ml water
50g Parmesan, grated
125ml single cream
Crème fraîche and black pepper,
  to garnish

TIPS & USES
● Select a medium-size pumpkin; they're generally sweeter than large ones. Cut the pumpkin in half and again into quarters and scrape out the seeds. (Roast the seeds and eat them as a snack.) Take care to keep the flat side down when cutting into it; if you cut with the round side down, it can rock and you can very easily cut yourself.

● Pumpkins keep for up to 3 months, providing stem and skin are left intact.

1 Preheat the oven to 180°C/gas mark 5.

2 Cut the pumpkin into quarters. Brush with olive oil and sprinkle with a small amount of salt. Roast for 1 hour, give or take 10 minutes, depending on the thickness of the pumpkin. It is best overdone, to allow the sweetness to develop.

3 Let the pumpkin cool for a few minutes, then scoop the flesh into a blender along with the lemon zest.

4 Using a pestle and mortar, grind up the caraway seeds and add them to the blender. Add 100ml of warm water and blend. You can adjust the consistency to your liking by adding more or less water, but I do prefer mine served thick. Add the cream.

5 Either pop this in the fridge to use later (it will keep for 3 days) or transfer it back to the stove and serve hot. It's important not to add the Parmesan until you're ready to eat as this gives you the option of using it in the next recipe: Pumpkin Pie. Just before serving stir in grated Parmesan. Garnish with a dollop of crème fraîche and salt and pepper to taste.

LINK
> Use the soup as the base for Pumpkin Pie on page 187. HOWEVER, you MUST exclude the Parmesan!

Pumpkin Pie

Makes 1 large pie to serve 8 people
Prep time 20 minutes, plus 30 minutes
for chilling
Cooking time 35 minutes

For the pastry
250g plain flour
  (00 is good but not essential)
Pinch of salt
50g icing sugar
125g butter
2 egg yolks
30ml ice-cold water

For the filling
200g caster sugar
800ml Caraway & Lemon Pumpkin Soup **>**
3 eggs
1 tsp caraway seeds

LINK
> Use Caraway & Lemon Pumpkin
Soup as the pie base: page 184.

1 Preheat the oven to 170°C/gas mark 3.

2 Sift the flour, salt and icing sugar into a mixing
bowl. Cut the butter into cubes in the flour, then rub
between the fingertips until the mixture resembles
fine breadcrumbs. Don't overdo this. Keep your
fingers deliberately light; it is essential to keep the
mixture as cold as possible for the best texture.

3 Add the egg yolks and a little of the water and
mix into a firm dough with a metal spoon. Use
your judgment with the water: add a few drops
at a time and mix; a few drops too many can
make the pastry too wet.

4 When the dough comes together, quickly use
your hands to form it into a ball. Wrap it in cling
film and allow it to rest in the refrigerator for
30 minutes before using.

5 Roll out onto a floured board and use to line
a 26cm quiche dish.

6 Put the sugar, soup base and eggs into a bowl
and mix well. Pour into the pastry-lined dish.
Scatter with a teaspoon of caraway seeds and
bake in the oven for 35 minutes.

TIPS & USES
● Both the pastry and the pumpkin mixture will
keep in the fridge for 48 hours, so when you're
ready to complete it, simply pour the base into
the pastry case and bake.

● If the pumpkin base is very cold, add an extra
5 minutes to the cooking time.

● You can use butternut squash in place of
pumpkin for the same result.

Caraway & Lemon Potato Cakes

This linked recipe goes with the Caraway & Lemon Chicken Pasties on page 191. It makes easy cooking and delicious eating, with very little clearing up for the second meal. Make the potato cakes to serve with Lemon Roast Chicken, then use the leftover chicken and half of the Caraway & Lemon Potato Cakes mix to make fragrant, buttery, lemon-infused pasties. Just pop leftover chopped chicken straight in with the potatoes and leave it in the fridge overnight. The following day you can have pasties in the oven in minutes with just one bowl to wash up. Fabulous food in a jiffy!

Serves 6 (2 potato cakes each)
Prep time 20 minutes
Cooking time 30 minutes
Suitable for freezing

You will need 100g of the mixture per potato cake. This recipe makes 12 potato cakes and leaves 400g left over to use for the pasties the following day.

1.2kg floury potatoes, such as
  Maris Piper, peeled
120g butter
1 level tbsp caraway seeds
200g grated Parmesan
Zest of 2 lemons
2 eggs
Sea salt
Black pepper
4–5 tbsp breadcrumbs
Oil, for frying

1 Put the peeled potatoes in a large saucepan, cover them with water and boil for 20 minutes. Drain, pop them back into the pan and add the butter, caraway, Parmesan, zest and just 1 of the eggs. Mash well and season with salt and pepper to taste. Remove about 400g to use for Caraway & Lemon Chicken Pasties.

2 Using your hands, form the potato mixture into 12 equal patties.

3 Beat the remaining egg and put it in a saucer. Put the breadcrumbs into another saucer and gently dip the patties first into the egg, then into the breadcrumbs.

4 Heat the oil in a heavy-based pan and fry the patties until golden brown. Serve immediately, but be careful not to over-handle them.

> **LINKS**
> > Lemon Roast Chicken, page 101
> > Caraway & Lemon Chicken Pasties, page 191

Caraway & Lemon Chicken Pasties

This follows on from the Caraway & Lemon Potato Cakes recipe on page 188, so be sure to make the potato mix first. For extra lemony zing, make these using leftover Lemon Roast Chicken from page 101.

Makes 6 pasties
Prep time 10 minutes
Cooking time 20 minutes
Suitable for freezing

260g leftover roast chicken, chopped
400g Caraway & Lemon Potato
 Cake mix **>**
500g shortcrust pastry
 (bought is fine)
1 egg, beaten, for glazing

1 Preheat the oven to 175°C/gas mark 4.

2 In a bowl, mix the chopped chicken thoroughly with the Caraway & Lemon Potato Cake mixture.

3 Roll out the pastry and divide it into 6 squares. Hold a pastry square in the palm of your hand, pop a dollop of about 110g of the mixture onto the centre of the pastry and use your free hand to fold up the sides to form a parcel. Pinch the seams together to seal. While holding the pasty, use your fingers to make it rounder, then gently place the parcel crease-side down.

4 You can set these to one side for a day or freeze them at this point, if you wish. To cook, turn the pasties over, cut a 2.5cm incision in the top of each and glaze the top with egg.

5 Put on a baking tray and bake in the oven for 20 minutes, or until golden brown. Allow to cool for 10 minutes before transferring them to a wire rack.

LINKS
> Lemon Roast Chicken, page 101
> Use the potato cake mix as topping for
Neapolitan Casa Pie: page 145.

Caraway Pork Balls & Caraway Sticky Rice Balls with Green Beans

Caramelised pork balls are quite simply fabulous. Get prepped by making double and freezing them, or use the pork-ball base to make burgers. When you bite through them, the first sensation is the crunch, then you're into succulent, juicy meat followed by the caraway. Dense, sweet, sticky rice balls are really worth the effort of making at the same time. The rice is sweetened on the outside, moist in the middle – providing a contrasting texture. Green beans add a final crunch and use the flavours left in the pan.

Caraway Pork Balls

Serves 4
Prep time 15 minute for each recipe;
30 minutes in total
Cooking time 12 minutes
Suitable for freezing Prior to cooking

1 onion, finely chopped
2 garlic cloves, finely sliced
3 tbsp wok oil
450g minced pork
80g breadcrumbs
6 tbsp sliced almonds
Pinch of salt
1 level tsp ground nutmeg
1 heaped tbsp caraway seeds
1 egg
1 chilli, finely chopped
5 heaped tbsp plain flour

1 Sauté the onion and garlic lightly.

2 Place all the ingredients except the flour into a bowl and mix together well. Form into golf-ball-size balls and roll in the flour.

3 In a large pan or wok, heat the wok oil on a low to medium heat. Cook the pork balls in the wok oil for about 12 minutes. You must make sure they are cooked all the way through. By keeping the pan temperature moderate you will caramelise the pork so that it is crispy on the outside and succulent inside. Not too hot or they will burn. Not too cool or they will be greasy. Try not to throw them around the pan using a spatula or they'll break up. Just shake the pan to roll them around gently.

Caraway Sticky Rice Balls

500g sushi rice
6 cardamom pods
1 medium onion, finely chopped
2 tbsp caraway seeds
Pinch of salt and white pepper
3 garlic cloves, very finely chopped

1 Cook the rice according to the packet instructions but add the cardamom pods to the water. Once cold, remove the cardamom pods; they've done their job.

2 Using the same pan or wok as you used for the pork, sauté the onion in the heated wok oil.

3 Add all the other ingredients and mix well. Moisten your hands with water and form into golf-ball-size balls. Follow the method of cooking as above for the pork balls.

Green Beans

150g green beans

Top and tail the beans, wash them, then cook together with extra garlic in the oil left over in the pan from the pork balls for 5–7 minutes.

LINK
> Use the Caraway Pork Ball base to make burgers instead: page 195.

TIP
● To serve, scatter all of the dishes with finely chopped chillies and Greek basil, and marigold petals if you have any in the garden.

Venison Burgers with Spiced Apple

It's a delight to pick apples from the tree in my garden, walk into the kitchen and cook them. And the venison is a treat: it's tender and surprisingly juicy, considering it's a low-fat meat. Apart from being utterly delicious, venison is a healthy option because it is low in saturated fat yet high in protein and iron. It's ideal for people who want to watch their cholesterol but still enjoy good red meat occasionally. Coupled with the caraway and the slightly tart spiced apple, it makes a light, fresh-tasting burger, and the apple complements the natural richness of the venison perfectly.

Serves 4
Prep time 15 minutes
Cooking time 6–10 minutes, depending on how well-cooked you like your burgers
Suitable for freezing Prior to cooking

For the spiced apple
250g cooking apple, cubed
30ml Lemon Syrup **>**
  or 30g caster sugar
Juice of 1 lemon
1 tbsp garam masala

For the burgers
500g minced venison
4 tbsp breadcrumbs
1 tbsp caraway seeds
3 tbsp Worcestershire sauce
Large pinch of salt

To serve
Baps (bought)
Salad to dress

1 To make the spiced apple, place all the ingredients in a pan over a low heat and cook gently for about 3 minutes. Don't be tempted to overdo it: you're looking for firm chunks, not mush. The mixture will continue to cook even as you take it off the heat, so leave the lid on and the apples will soften further without losing their shape.

2 Meanwhile, put all the ingredients for the burgers into a bowl and mix together well. Form into 4 equal-sized patties but squeeze the meat together gently in the shape of a burger. Because of its low fat content, venison doesn't shrink in the same way beef does, so make sure your patties are the right size for the baps.

3 Cook your burgers under a medium-hot grill for about 2–3 minutes each side. I like mine rare, but judge how you like your meat. Whatever you do, don't keep flipping your burgers; these are homemade and need to be treated gently, so just cook one side and turn to cook the other.

4 Place the burgers onto the baps with a handful of salad, top with spiced apple and serve immediately.

TIP
● Use pork or beef instead of venison – but be sure to cook pork all the way through.

LINKS
> Lemon Syrup, page 82
> Try Spiced Tomato Jam (page 128) if apples aren't available.
> Use the Caraway Pork Ball mix to make the burgers: page 192.

Caraway Soda Bread

One of the fastest baking tricks on the planet. I challenge anyone to take more than five minutes flat to get this bread into the oven. Make no mistake: the speed doesn't mean you're compromising on taste. On the contrary, the pace of its creation should be counterbalanced by the speed of eating it – which is best soon after baking. Every now and then I like to grab a fast breakfast with friends straight from the school run. For me, it's perfect timing to throw this bread in the oven just before I leave the house. Twenty-five minutes later I'm back. The kitchen is filled with the smell of fresh baking and the air with aromatic caraway. As you slice the crunchy crust you'll notice that the warm dough is dense. It has a solid, satisfying texture to it. Still warm, dripping with butter and smothered in plum jam, it's best served with a good, strong cup of hot tea – and a smidgen of gossip.

Makes 1 good-size loaf
Prep time 4 minutes
Cooking time 25–30 minutes
Suitable for freezing As soon as it's cool from the oven

500g plain flour
1½ tsp caster sugar
1 tsp baking soda
1 tsp sea salt
1 tbsp caraway seeds
450ml buttermilk

TIPS & USES

● Soak a tablespoon of dried lavender in warm buttermilk for 15 minutes and add to the dough with 3 tbsp of extra sugar for a sweetened lavender bread.

● Add the zest of 2 lemons and 2 tablespoons of poppy seeds for a lemon and poppy seed loaf.

● Make a savoury tea loaf by adding 100g of raisins.

● Double the recipe to freeze a batch.

● Double the recipe and use it to make Caraway Scones: page 175.

1 Preheat the oven to190°C/gas mark 5 a good 10 minutes before you start making the bread.

2 Sift all the dry ingredients into a large mixing bowl

3 Add the buttermilk. Mix well but don't overmix. It will go claggy and heavy if handled too much.

4 Turn the bread out into a lightly oiled bread tin.

5 Bake in the oven for approximately 25–30 minutes. Check to see whether the loaf is baked by slipping a knife into the centre. If it comes out clean, then it is done; if not, then return it to the oven for another 5 minutes and check again. When the loaf is baked all the way though it sounds hollow when tapped on the bottom.

6 Serve warm from the oven.

LINKS
> Makes an ideal accompaniment to Pear, Walnut & Beetroot Salad, page 21.
> Serve with Rhubarb Jam or Plum Jam: pages 40 and 160.
> Delightful as a partner for Mackerel & Dill Pâté: page 43.

Caraway Biscotti

Time is precious. So when you get the chance to sit and have a moment with a friend, it needs to be extra special. It's not as difficult as you might think. Just a few minutes and a natter shared with one of these biscotti over a cup of coffee is such a treat. They are light and sophisticated, memorable and altogether moreish. Which is what we want: moreish time to catch up with friends.

Makes 30–35
Prep time 20 minutes
Cooking time 35 minutes
Suitable for freezing After the first baking

300g whole almonds
200g granulated sugar
400g self-raising flour
1 level tsp coarse sea salt
1 tsp baking powder
6 large eggs
2 tbsp caraway seeds

TIPS & USES

● Please use a heavy-duty food mixer such a Kenwood or KitchenAid. This dough is very stiff and a hand-held mixer will not cope with the strain on the motor!

● To avoid the biscuit breaking apart as you cut through the almonds, don't 'saw'! Instead, use a very sharp knife and cut straight down, with the heel of your hand pressing down on the top of the knife.

● These make a lovely gift – at any time of year.

1 Preheat the oven to 180°C/gas mark 4.

2 To add a good crunch to the almonds, gently dry-toast them in a heavy-based frying pan. Take care, though, as they burn easily.

3 In a bowl mix the sugar, flour, salt and baking powder together.

4 Beat the eggs in a mixing bowl or food processor, then slowly add the dry mix to form a loose dough. Add the roasted almonds and caraway seeds at the end, and stir them in gently; you don't want to break them up.

5 Form the mixture into 2 logs approximately 25cm inches long and no more than 10cm wide. Transfer the mixture to a large, greased baking tray, but leave a gap between the logs because they expand. Bake for 20–25 minutes. Remove from the oven and cool.

6 Now cut the logs into individual biscuits. Using a sharp knife, cut each log into 2cm portions (you can freeze them at this point) and return the slices to the oven. Toast for 10–12 minutes on each side. Don't be tempted to overcook them.

7 Transfer the biscotti to a wire rack and leave them to dry out completely for 1–2 hours, then transfer to an airtight container.

LINK
> For a festive Christmas twist, omit the caraway and replace the caster sugar with Orange & Clove Sugar: page 245.

Chocolate

If chocolate were a musical chord it would be played at the base end of a piano. There is no doubt whatsoever that this wonderful food works (impeccably!) as a sweet in its own right, but even when it isn't centre-stage, the presence of chocolate adds intrigue and complexity to the foundation layers of a dish.

Aligning it with deep, rich flavours such as venison, for example, yields a rich tone and imparts a sometimes unidentifiable deliciousness to these savoury foods. There is also a depth to dark chocolate that complements the low tones under beef or over exotic dishes such as Chilli Chocolate Cake.

Rich, dark, intense; sweet, creamy, fragrant; melt-in-the-mouth, smooth… whichever way you enjoy chocolate, this flavour has a lot more to offer than luxurious after-dinner indulgence from the dessert trolley.

Savoury Chocolate Biscuits

The chocolate in these biscuits takes a supporting role rather than occupying centre-stage. As a savoury cheese biscuit this has almost a shortbread quality about it, crunching and crumbling before melting into a sublime combination of buttery dark, salted chocolate with just a hint of heat behind it. When paired with a mellow Cheddar they are quite simply moreish.

Makes about 25
Prep time 15 minutes, plus 1 hour to chill
Cooking time 12 minutes
Suitable for freezing Prior to baking

220g plain 00 flour
½ tsp paprika
Pinch of salt
4 tbsp cocoa powder
1 tsp baking powder
2 tbsp Cardamom Sugar >
60g dark chocolate
    (70% cocoa solids), grated
145g butter
2 eggs
75g poppy seeds

1 Sift the flour, paprika, salt, cocoa powder and baking powder into a bowl. Add the Cardamom Sugar and grated chocolate and combine.

2 Rub in the butter until the mixture resembles breadcrumbs, then add just 1 egg and mix to form a soft dough.

3 On a floured surface roll out the dough into a large sausage. Beat the second egg, then brush the sausage with it before rolling it on a tray sprinkled with the poppy seeds. Transfer the log to the fridge for an hour to chill.

4 Preheat the oven to 160°C/gas mark 3.

5 Using a sharp knife, slice the log in disks about 5mm thick before transferring onto a tray lined with baking paper. Bake for about 12 minutes. Don't be tempted to overdo them, however: they won't set properly until they are cold.

TIPS & USES
● Put half the log away in the freezer to use another time.

● Store in an airtight container for up to a week.

● For a pretty finish, roll the biscuits in sesame seeds.

● Wrap in cellophane with a beautiful hunk of Cheddar to make a cracking gift for cheese-loving men-folk!

● To transform them into sweet biscuits, add 75g of sugar and increase the butter by 20g.

LINKS
> Cardamom Sugar, page 226
> Serve with Cardamom Honey Drizzle Fig Salad and cheese, page 230.

Chocolate Beef

Eating chocolate in a meat dish may not be the first thing to spring to mind if you think of chocolate, but I'm sure that once you've tried this recipe, you'll find yourself adding it to lamb or venison in much the same way. This is a savoury/sweet combination with a difference. You don't taste the chocolate; it sits under the gravy, quite unidentifiable but utterly intriguing, and this dish is all the more delicious because of it. The beef is richer, with added warmth and depth. With its spicy overtones and sweet undertones, this melt-in-your-mouth casserole is a perfect choice for supper guests. And the leftovers make fabulous pasties.

Serves 4–6
Prep time 15 minutes
Cooking time 3 hours
Suitable for freezing

2 tbsp rapeseed or olive oil
2 banana shallots or mild onions,
   finely chopped
1kg shin of beef, diced
3 star anise
5 cloves
4 celery sticks
4 large carrots
1 x 400g tin plum tomatoes
500ml water
Half a bottle fruity red wine
1½ tsp sea salt
50g dark 60% cocoa chocolate

1 Preheat the oven to 175°C/gas mark 4.

2 Heat the oil in a heavy-based pan that can go in the oven with a lid. Sauté the shallots or onion until lightly browned, then add the diced beef a handful at a time and sauté until brown.

3 Add the star anise and the cloves. Pop the celery and carrots in the pan whole. Add the tomatoes and water and stir well.

4 Pour in the wine and salt, stir well and transfer the pot to the oven. Cook for 1 hour.

5 Remove the pan from the oven and stir in the chocolate. Don't be tempted to add more – trust me: too much is overkill! Return the pan to the oven and cook for a further 2 hours. Allow to cool for a few minutes, discard the celery and carrots, and serve with creamy mashed potato.

TIPS & USES

● For a bit of colour, garnish the beef with some marigold petals from the garden.

● Add ½ teaspoon of paprika if you want to 'heat it up'; it works beautifully.

● Substitute a good stout instead of the red wine for a more gastro-pub-type result.

> **LINK**
> > Use the beef to make Chocolate Beef Pasties;
>   see page 191 for the method.

Chocolate Cookie Mix

Why buy cookie mixes from the shops when it's so easy to make this one yourself? Of course, these jars make super gifts, but keep one handy in the cupboard and you can have dark, rich and melt-in-the-mouth chocolate cookies on the table in 20 minutes flat for half the cost of bought ones!

Makes 24
Prep time 10 minutes
Cooking time 10–12 minutes

For the mix
220g self-raising flour
Pinch of salt
120g dark brown sugar
130g caster sugar
45g cocoa powder
60g roughly chopped walnuts
150g chopped dark chocolate

120g soft butter
1 egg

1 Sift the flour into a bowl. Add the salt.

2 In another bowl, mix the dark brown sugar and the caster sugar together. Make sure it is well-mixed – this stops the brown sugar from clumping.

3 Layer the flour, cocoa powder and sugar into a 1-litre jar with an airtight seal. Add the walnuts and chocolate on top and close well. (Note: if you're giving this as a gift, you can hand-write a label with the instructions in steps 4–6 below.)

4 To make the cookies, preheat the oven to 175°C/gas mark 4. Tip the contents of the jar into a mixing bowl or food processor. Add the butter and the egg and mix for 2–3 minutes, until the ingredients are well-blended.

5 Use your hands to roll the dough into walnut-size pieces. Pop them on a lightly greased baking sheet.

6 Bake for 10–12 minutes. Remove the tray from the oven and leave the cookies for a few minutes to allow the chocolate to set a little before transferring them to a wire wrack to cool completely.

TIPS & USES
● Replace the chopped chocolate with raisins for a fruity, chewy finish to the cookies.

● Substitute milk or white chocolate for the dark chocolate.

LINKS
> To change flavours, use Lavender, Vanilla, Cardamom or Orange & Clove sugars (see pages 58, 108, 226 and 245) instead of caster sugar.

Chocolate & Vanilla Whoopie Pies

Here you have a taste of America: 16 Chocolate & Vanilla Whoopie Pies! The chocolate-and-vanilla combination is terrific at the best of times, but when biscuity chocolate cake is sandwiched around soft folds of whipped vanilla cream, it is heaven. 'Whoopie pies' originated from the Amish people in Pennsylvania, USA. Apparently, wives made these chocolate mounds with butter icing sandwiched between them for their husbands. The husbands were so pleased they shouted, 'Whoopie!' I understand completely!

Makes 16
Prep time 20 minutes
Cooking time 10 minutes
Suitable for freezing Before filling

For the pies
280g self-raising flour
4 large heaped tbsp cocoa powder
Pinch of salt
200g caster sugar
120g butter
1 tsp vanilla extract
2 medium eggs
250ml buttermilk

For the filling
1 level tsp vanilla paste
3 tbsp icing sugar
300ml double cream

1 Preheat the oven to 180°C/gas mark 4. Grease 2 baking trays.

2 Combine the flour, cocoa powder and salt in a mixing bowl. In a separate bowl, beat the sugar, butter and vanilla until pale and fluffy, then add the eggs. Mix well.

3 Add the dry ingredients and buttermilk to the egg mixture and mix well. You should be left with a relatively stiff mixture ready to spoon onto the baking tray in round, bite-sized blobs. To get 16 pies you will need 32 of these.

4 Bake in the oven for 10–12 minutes. They should come out as a cross between a biscuit and a sponge; however, PAY ATTENTION: there is a fine line between biscuit and burned because of this recipe's high sugar content, so don't leave them in too long! Transfer them to a wire rack to cool.

5 To make the filling, add the teaspoon of vanilla paste and icing sugar to the cream and whip. Make sure the cream is a nice thick consistency before sandwiching a dollop between 2 chocolate cakes.

LINKS
> Use Lavender, Vanilla or Cardamom Sugar instead of plain caster sugar (see pages 58, 108 or 226).
> For a super-rich filling, use the Chocolate Truffle Ganache (page 212).

TIPS & USES
● Any good-quality vanilla paste will do for this recipe; however, I prefer Fairtrade and organic types such as Ndali.

● You can create endless flavour combinations to vary this recipe. Try infusing cardamom, orange or lavender into the cream to add an instant extra layer.

Double Cook: Chocolate Truffles and Chocolate, Cardamom & Orange Gelato

I just LOVE this recipe. This is a one-pot cook: one shop, one lot of clearing up and two fabulous chocolate results. The Gelato is made by leaving half the ganache in the bowl, popping it over a saucepan of hot water, adding egg yolks and milk and stirring. That's it! You have ice cream and the ganache ready to make your truffles with – and NO extra washing up. Now that's my kind of cooking!

Step 1: Chocolate Truffle Ganache

Let's demystify the truffle. Truffles are simply firm ganache – and ganache is just melted chocolate and cream. As far as linked recipes and flavour layers are concerned, ganache gets you well and truly prepped for this and the recipe that follows, and it can be substituted for icings and fillings in a number of others. These truffles make superb gifts that have an air of sophistication, and they can be kept for up to six weeks in the fridge. Perfect prepped presents!

Makes 36 truffles & 8 servings of gelato
Prep time 10 minutes
Cooking time 30–40 minutes in total

500g plain chocolate
300ml double cream
80g glucose syrup
100g cold butter
6 tbsp cocoa powder,
    to roll the truffles in

LINKS
> Chocolate, Cardamom & Orange Gelato, page 215
> Use the Ganache as the filling for Chilli Chocolate Cupcakes: page 216.
> Use the Ganache as the topping for the Chocolate & Raspberry Cake, page 221.

1 Break up the chocolate into small pieces and place these in a large heatproof bowl that fits comfortably over a saucepan.

2 In another saucepan, heat the cream and glucose over a low heat until it is just on the point of boiling. Pour into the bowl of chocolate and stir from the middle to get a smooth, thick, shiny emulsion.

3 Leave the mixture to cool. If you have a cooking thermometer, it needs to cool to about 35–40°C. If you don't have a thermometer, leave the mixture to cool for 5 minutes until it reaches skin temperature.

4 Chop the butter into 2.5cm squares, add these to the chocolate mixture and, using a hand mixer on its lowest setting, mix in well. You're looking to thicken the mixture using the hand mixer, but it's important not to let any air bubbles in. Gently! Gently!

5 Remove half the ganache and put it into an airtight container to allow it to set to room temperature before using – it should be thick. Now continue using the remaining ganache to make the gelato recipe on page 215.

Step 2: Chocolate, Cardamom & Orange Gelato

This is about as deep and rich as an ice cream can be. It keeps happily for up to three months in the freezer – if you can leave it alone that long!

Half quantity of Chocolate
  Truffle Ganache >
4 egg yolks
75g Cardamom Sugar >
Zest of 1 orange
600ml whole milk

TIPS & USES

● Layer flavour into your truffles. Before making the ganache, steep lavender, vanilla, the rind of a lemon or an orange, or 6–7 cardamom pods in the cream overnight. This imparts your chosen flavour to the cream, giving you intense, handmade truffles at the drop of a hat.

● Instead of pouring all the mixture into the ice-cream mixer, pour some into espresso cups and leave them to set in the fridge – they make extraordinarily rich, sumptuous chocolate treats and keep for up to 3 days covered in cling film.

1 Put the Chocolate Truffle Ganache in a heatproof bowl on top of a saucepan that is a third full of hot water.

2 Add the egg yolks, sugar and orange zest to the bowl. Mix these into the ganache and slowly add the milk. Whisk gently to mix the ingredients, then transfer the saucepan to the hob and bring the water in the pan up to a gentle boil. Keep stirring; this is very important!

3 Once the water is boiling, keep it at a quiet boil and stir until the mixture thickens enough to coat the back of a spoon easily. This takes about 15 minutes, so be patient.

4 Set the large bowl aside to cool completely. Then, transfer the mixture to your ice-cream maker and follow the instructions for your particular machine. Alternatively, if you're making this by hand, pour the mixture into a shallow freezer-proof container, freeze for about 1 hour, then whisk it every 35 minutes or so for 3–4 times total to prevent ice crystals forming and get a smooth result. (Use your mobile phone alarm to remind you; I often forget to go back and whisk!)

5 You can now return to the remaining half of the ganache and make the truffles at your leisure. The mix needs to be firm and not too warm. Use a melon baller to scoop out balls of ganache. Roll each briefly in the palm of your hand, then drop it into a bowl containing 6 tbsp sifted cocoa powder. That's it: easy!

6 Mine keep in the fridge in an airtight container for up to 6 weeks – but to be fair, I had to hide them at the back to test this theory!

LINKS
> Chocolate Truffle Ganache, page 212
> Cardamom Sugar, page 226.

Chilli Chocolate Cupcakes

These cupcakes are designed for grown-ups only. You get your sweet fix, followed by a chilli hit and an intense chocolate burst to finish – just how I like it! It is a rich batter, though, so one is generally enough. A word of warning: don't use pickled beetroot! I love the fact that, by making the filling for these, I have also made a batch of chocolate truffles at the same time. It's such a bonus for no extra washing up!

Makes 18
Prep time 10 minutes for the cakes,
15 minutes for decoration
Cooking time 25 minutes
Suitable for freezing
Before decorating

For the cupcakes
225g self-raising flour
75g cocoa powder
1 level tsp chilli powder
280g caster sugar
1 tsp bicarbonate of soda
3 eggs
150ml rapeseed oil
300g cooked beetroot (plain, not
   pickled), grated and drained

For the filling
225g Chocolate Truffle Ganache **>**
   (half the recipe from page 212)

For the chillies
2 small packets of florist's icing paste:
   1 red, 1 green

For the icing
White of 1 egg
200g icing sugar
3 tbsp cocoa powder

1 Preheat the oven to 180°C/gas mark 4.

2 Sift all the dry ingredients for the cake into a bowl.

3 In a separate bowl place the 3 eggs and whisk. Add the oil and beetroot.

4 Add the dry mixture to the wet ingredients. Mix well.

5 Line a muffin tin with 18 large cupcake papers/ muffin paper cases and divide the mixture among them, filling each case two-thirds full. Bake for 25 minutes, or until they have risen and spring back into shape if touched.

6 Leave to cool completely on a wire rack.

7 While the cupcakes are in the oven, break off small pieces of the red sugar paste, roll them in your hands to a chewing gum consistency, then roll each into a chilli shape. Work quickly; otherwise the paste will dry out, so keep what you're not using well-covered. Make 'stalks' using the green paste. Using the end of a chopstick, push a small dent in the top of each 'chilli' and, using a really tiny drop of water as glue, stick the two together. Voilà: you're now ready to top your cakes with chillies!

8 Gently cut a piece out of the centre of each cupcake to make a 'hat', then pinch out some of the soft inner cake from the bottom of the 'hat' to make space for the filling.

9 Half-fill the centre of each cupcake with Chocolate Ganache – or a filling of your choice. Place the 'hat' back on each.

TIPS & USES

● Instead of cupcakes, make 1 large cake, slice it through the middle, then spread Chocolate Truffle Ganache in the centre.

● Keep the cake whole, make the Chocolate Truffle Ganache just before serving and pour it over hot as a pudding.

● You can use packaged cooked beetroot – just not the type steeped in vinegar!

10 To make the icing, mix the egg white, cocoa powder and icing sugar together in a bowl. Adjust the consistency to get a good, thick icing and spread this generously on top of each cupcake to hide the cut-out. Top each with a sugar 'chilli' and serve.

LINKS

> Use Chocolate Truffle Ganache from page 212 as the filling. I make the full recipe and use the leftovers to make a batch of chocolate truffles at the same time.

Chocolate & Almond Pavlova Cake

This fantastical cake looks seriously impressive, but the truth is that it is a cinch to make – and it tastes fabulous and has the added advantage of being gluten-free. It is not, however, the tidiest of cakes to serve, and it is very rich, but I can assure you that it is well worth putting up with the extra cholesterol and a few crumbs to eat it! The texture of the meringue has to be soft and marshmallow-like. Coupled with the rich, deep ganache and the soft, moist, brownie-type torte underneath, it is the sort of cake a princess would have – albeit a messy-eating princess!

Serves 8
Prep time 20 minutes
Cooking time 1 hour 5 minutes

For the cake
170g butter, softened, plus extra
  for greasing
200g dark chocolate, broken
100g caster sugar
A few drops vanilla extract
6 medium eggs, separated
100g ground almonds

2 Pavlova meringue bases **>**
  (make the same recipe, but divide the
  mixture into 2 circles instead of 1)

For the chocolate ganache
220g dark chocolate
200ml double cream

For the filling
500ml whipped cream

For decoration
40g melted chocolate
30g toasted hazelnuts

1 Preheat the oven to 170°C/gas mark 3.

2 Grease a 20cm springform cake tin with butter. Dust with flour.

3 Put the chocolate in a bowl over a pan of hot water and melt. Be careful not to let the bowl touch the water. It will ruin the chocolate by getting too hot. Allow the chocolate to cool slightly.

4 Meanwhile, cream the butter with the sugar until pale and fluffy. Fold in the melted chocolate, vanilla extract, egg yolks and the ground almonds.

5 Whip the egg whites until stiff. Stir about a third into the batter first, to loosen the mix; this makes it easier to fold in the rest. Spoon into the cake tin.

6 Bake for 20 minutes, then reduce the oven to 150°C/gas mark 2 and bake for a further 45 minutes.

7 Remove the cake from the oven and allow it to rest for a few minutes. Cool in the tin on a wire rack for about 15 minutes before removing to cool completely on the wire rack.

8 To make the ganache: melt the chocolate as above. Bring the cream to a boil in a small pan, then stir into the chocolate. Beat this until glossy. Cool slightly.

9 Make the meringue bases by following the recipe on page 44, but split the mixture into 2 circles instead of 1.

10 When you're ready to make the pavlova, start with 1 meringue, slather this with a good layer of chocolate ganache and whipped cream. Place the torte on top, slather it again with ganache and cream and top with the remaining meringue.

11 To decorate, drizzle melted chocolate over the top of the cake and scatter with hazelnuts.

TIPS & USES

● For a symmetrical cake, use a couple of 24cm rubber cake moulds for the meringues. However, I prefer a slightly more 'artistic' approach and use a pencil to draw a circle 4cm smaller than the torte on greaseproof paper. I turn this over and dollop the meringue mixture onto these. The circles need to be smaller to take into account the fact that meringue rises and expands in the oven.

● The chocolate cake alone is utterly delicious if you haven't got the time to make the pavlova.

LINKS
> Rhubarb Pavlova (for the meringue recipe), page 44
> If you use half the Chocolate Truffle Ganache recipe from page 212, you can use the other half to make truffles with for zero effort!

LINKS

> Chocolate Truffle Ganache (page 212) makes a serious chocolate statement, both glossy and rich, instead of the icing given here.

Chocolate & Raspberry Cake

Now I'm guessing vinegar, cream cheese and sea salt aren't the kind of ingredients most people expect to find in a chocolate cake. Trust me on this one: I don't do sickly sweet chocolate. Instead, this cake is deep, rich and resonating with dark chocolate and fruity raspberry tones. It's straightforward to make and a real showpiece, so if you have people to impress, this dessert will do just that.

Serves 10
Prep time 20 minutes
Cooking time 1 hour
Suitable for freezing
Before decorating

For the cake
250ml milk
3 tbsp balsamic vinegar
160g dark chocolate
100g butter
30g cocoa powder
300g self-raising flour, sifted
1 tsp bicarbonate of soda, sifted
125g dark muscovado sugar
100g caster sugar
2 eggs
Pinch of sea salt

For the icing
125g dark chocolate
  (minimum 60% cocoa solids)
50g butter
75ml double cream

For the filling
150ml double cream
70g cream cheese
1 medium punnet of fresh raspberries

TIP
● Use strawberries instead of raspberries. Personally I'd throw in blueberries as well to haul in the sweetness.

1 Preheat the oven to 180°C/gas mark 4. Grease a 24cm round, deep cake tin and line it with baking paper.

2 Mix the milk and vinegar together. Set aside.

3 Melt the chocolate and butter using a bain-marie or a heatproof bowl placed over a saucepan of simmering water, then pour into a large mixing bowl. Add all the other ingredients and mix well.

4 Pour in the milk mixture and beat with an electric hand whisk until it forms a smooth batter.

5 Pour into the cake tin and bake for 1 hour, or until it is firm in the centre. Test for doneness by inserting a knife in the centre; if it comes out clean, it's ready; if not, then return the cake to the oven for 5–10 minutes and repeat the test.

6 Cool for 10–15 minutes in the tin, then turn out onto a wire rack to cool completely.

7 Meanwhile, make the icing. Melt the chocolate and butter in a bain-marie or in a heatproof bowl placed over a pan of simmering water. Stir well until smooth, then beat in the cream. Allow this to cool a little, but not completely; it should be thick and yet still viscous.

8 Whip the cream and cream cheese together for the filling, taking care not to make it too thick.

9 Cut the cake in half through the middle, place the bottom half on a cake stand or plate and cover it with the cream cheese mixture. Arrange the raspberries on top of this, then place the top half of the cake on the raspberries. Pour the icing over the top.

Chocolate, Vanilla & Black Pepper Cupcakes

Enough is enough sometimes, you just have to have a treat. Something extravagant. I love that this recipe contains rapeseed oil because I feel that the health benefits of this balance out the naughtiness of the cream! These dark, rich, chocolate cupcakes are filled with voluptuous whipped cream flavoured with black pepper to create a spiced eastern backdrop, while the vanilla sings over the top with its sweet, high notes. Heaven!

Makes 18
Prep time 10 minutes for the cakes,
15 for decoration
Cooking time 25 minutes
Suitable for freezing
Before decorating

For the cupcakes
225g self-raising flour
75g cocoa powder
280g caster sugar
1 tsp bicarbonate of soda
3 eggs
150ml rapeseed oil
300g cooked beetroot, grated
  and drained

For the filling
450ml fresh double cream
4 tbsp icing sugar
2 tsp vanilla essence
About 20 grinds of fine black pepper
  (or 1 level tsp)

For decoration
About 25g chocolate shavings

1 Preheat the oven to 170°C/gas mark 3.

2 Sift all the dry ingredients for the cake into a bowl.

3 Put the 3 eggs in a separate bowl and whisk. Add the oil and beetroot.

4 Add the dry mixture to the wet ingredients. Mix well.

5 Line a muffin tin with 18 large cupcake/muffin paper cases and divide the mixture among them. Bake for 25 minutes, or until they have risen and spring back into shape if touched.

6 Leave to cool completely on a wire rack.

7 Whip the cream, icing sugar, vanilla essence and black pepper together until thick – be careful not to overdo the pepper. I suggest grinding some in then tasting until you are happy with the balance.

8 Gently cut a piece out of the centre of each cupcake to make a 'hat', then slice this in half. Fill the hole with the cream and pop the top back on the make 'wings'.

9 Scatter with chocolate shavings and serve. If you're not eating them straight away, these will keep in an airtight container until the use-by date of your cream.

LINKS
> The base of these cupcakes is the same as the Chilli Chocolate Cupcakes (page 216) – minus the chilli, of course!
> Use the cream in the Chocolate & Raspberry Cake on page 221.

Cardamom

Fragrant, exotic, romantic: cardamom reminds me of a Senegalese dancer I once lived with in Paris. Remove cardamom from its curry counterparts and you will find a deep, complex, highly versatile yet individual spice. With its ebony seeds encased in green, papery pods, cardamom's cleansing, camphorish qualities pirouette, like my friend the dancer, across your taste buds while its citrous tones balance the richness.

Mixed with other flavours it marries well to give some seriously beautiful combinations in your kitchen. Paired with chocolate, basil, vanilla or orange, cardamom's warmth and spice step up your game in so many dishes.

Cardamom Sugar

My favourite trick for turning the mundane into the interesting, Cardamom Sugar marries well with chocolate, vanilla, lemon, ginger, nutmeg and aniseed, to name but a few. This spice is one of those kitchen additions that will have your friends and family talking about your fabulous cooking (in between mouthfuls). Aromatic and mysterious, it works on both savoury and sweet fronts. Infusing cardamoms into the sugar over a few weeks results in the intensity of this flavour enveloping a recipe naturally instead of dominating it. Like sinking into a favourite armchair, it sits far more comfortably with the other ingredients.

Makes about 2kg
Prep time 5 minutes

2kg caster sugar
100g green cardamoms
1 x 2-litre jar, or several smaller ones to
    fit the sugar in (with tight-fitting lids)

1 Layer the sugar and cardamoms directly into the jars, dispersing them as evenly as possible throughout.

2 Seal and leave for at least a month, although 6 weeks is better if you can bear it!

TIPS & USES

● Use this sugar in custard to spice up an apple crumble, or use the custard for a trifle – which, incidentally, works really well if combined with ginger wine instead of sherry.

● If you add sugar to your tea or coffee, try this sugar instead.

● Use infused sugar to replace plain sugar in cakes, muffins, biscuits, shortbread and rice pudding. All are super cardamom candidates, so it's worth the effort of revisiting old favourites armed with a large jar. But do try the Victoria Sponge Cake with Cardamom, Rose Cream & Rhubarb (page 238) first!

● Buying cardamom in supermarkets is expensive. Discover your nearest Asian supermarket: spice heaven! Here most spices are double the quantity, half the price and generally, because of the high turnover, fresher than supermarket equivalents.

● Keep several jars running at once so that you have one 'brewing' as another is used.

● Replace the sugar as you use it up to three times; after that, you'll need to replace the cardamoms. Store any spare ones in a tightly sealed jam jar.

LINKS

> Use to add an extra dimension to Rhubarb Syrup, page 36.
> Use in place of regular sugar in 100mph Rhubarb & Cardamom Batter Cake (page 55); Lemon Cake (page 105); Vanilla Blondies (page 125) and Chocolate Cookie Mix (page 206).
> Use instead of Lavender Sugar in Lavender Shortbread (page 75) and Lavender & Lemon Cake (page 79).
> Use instead of Vanilla Sugar in Rice Pudding (page 121), Custard (page 118), and Crème Brûlée (page 122).
> Plum Cobbler, page 172
> Hot Chocolate with Cardamom Sugar, page 229
> Cardamom & Basil Ice Cream, page 234
> Victoria Sponge Cake with Cardamom Rose Cream & Rhubarb, page 238

Hot Chocolate with Cardamom Sugar

Perhaps it seems a little silly to include a recipe on how to make a hot chocolate, but the truth is there are so many instant packs and stuff with nasty ingredients out there that I think we tend to forget just how good an old-fashioned hot chocolate really tastes. So let me remind you. It's warm, velvety, sweet and dark, with a spiced undertone. It's a cuddle in a cup. Whenever I get cold, short of having a hot bath, this is what really warms me up.

Serves 1
Prep time 2 minutes

3 heaped teaspoons cocoa powder
2 heaped tsp Cardamom Sugar **>**
Splash of hot water to mix
200ml hot milk

1 In a mug, mix the cocoa powder and sugar together and add a splash of hot water to mix.

2 Slowly add the hot milk, stirring well. Serve immediately.

LINKS
> Substitute Lavender Sugar (page 58) for Cardamom Sugar to send you to sleep, or try Vanilla Sugar (page 108) instead. For a festive Christmas cup, use Orange & Clove Sugar and a good slug (25ml) of Orange & Clove Brandy (pages 245 and 242).
> Cardamom Sugar, page 226

Cardamom Honey Drizzle Fig Salad

I wondered about including this recipe. It's so uncomplicated that I almost feel there should be more to it. But there isn't. It's quite simply a gorgeous combination that goes together in minutes and is available to use as a starter, an accompaniment to cheese, or as a stand-alone salad. It really is a versatile little number.

Serves 4
Prep time 4 minutes
Cooking time 3 minutes

2 cardamom pods
3 tbsp honey
50g hazelnuts
1 packet of watercress
8 ripe figs

1 Break open the cardamom pods and drop them into a saucepan with the honey. Bring up to the boil for just a second, then remove the pan from the heat.

2 While the honey cools, toast the hazelnuts in the oven at 160°C /gas mark 3 for a few minutes to give them some crunch. Take care: they only need 3–4 minutes and burn easily. Arrange the watercress on a serving plate.

3 Slice the figs into quarters and lay them over the watercress. Scatter the hazelnuts over the figs.

4 Sieve the cooled honey and drizzle it over the figs just before serving.

LINKS
> Use the honey on Baked Goats Cheese: page 61.
> Serve with Savoury Chocolate Biscuits: page 202.

Cardamom & Orange Barfi

A while ago a fretful friend was trying to help her son choose a university. She asked how I chose mine (I think she was expecting a helpful answer!). Truth is, the reason I chose Leicester was because, at the time, it had more curry houses per square mile than anywhere else in the UK. One in particular stood out: Bobby's. I've been eating there since I was 12 and it's still the best. I have owner Darmish and his chef, Deepak, to thank for teaching me the basic barfi recipe. It's utterly moreish, is a brilliant after-dinner alternative to mints and makes a very different gift.

Makes 12 large pieces
Prep time 15 minutes
Cooking time 5 minutes

500g full-fat milk powder
200ml cold water
120g ghee (clarified butter)
200ml warm water
160g Cardamom Sugar **>**
1 tsp ground cardamom
   (or 8 cardamoms, finely ground)
Zest of 1 orange, finely grated
70g chopped pistachios and almonds

1 Wipe a baking tray lightly with vegetable oil, then line it with baking paper. Leave the paper slightly proud of the edges to make it easy to take out later.

2 Put the milk powder into a large bowl. In a large saucepan heat the cold water and 100g of the ghee. Once at boiling point, pour the water into the milk solids and mix well with a spoon. Use your hand to mix once the temperature has come down. Set aside.

3 Using the same saucepan, add the rest of the ghee, the warm water, sugar and the ground cardamom. Heat to dissolve the sugar. Turn the milk powder mix into the pan and add the orange zest. Mix well over a high heat for just 1 minute, stirring vigorously, then turn out onto the tray. Don't worry if it's a little lumpy; it will smooth out as it sets.

4 Scatter with roughly chopped nuts and leave to set for 4–5 hours. Remove from the tray and cut into shapes. Use within a week. Keep cool.

TIPS & USES

● Instead of cutting out squares, roll the dough into balls and coat them in chocolate. The result is like a spicy marzipan.

● Substitute lemon zest for orange zest.

> ### LINKS
> **>** Substitute Lavender Sugar (page 58) for the cardamom and Cardamom Sugar to make Lavender Barfi.
> **>** Cardamom Sugar, page 226

Cardamom & Basil Ice Cream

Initially I was making cardamom ice cream. As I tasted the custard (that's effectively what ice cream is) it seemed one-dimensional. Musing over how to enhance the taste and without really knowing why, I found myself whizzing up a handful of Greek basil from a pot on the window sill and throwing it into the ice-cream maker just as it started to churn. As the mixture turned green, the prickly thought arose that basil was a fairly odd thing to add and it could prove to be a disaster. I mean, come on: basil in ice cream? But my instincts were right. This is so refreshing after a heavy meal and quite possibly the nicest ice cream I've ever tasted.

Serves 10
Prep time 15 minutes
Cooking time 15 minutes, plus freezing time: allow 25 minutes for an ice-cream maker or 3–4 hours by hand

10 egg yolks
100ml double cream
200g Cardamom Sugar **>**
900ml skimmed milk
8 cardamom pods (optional)
5 stems of Greek basil

TIPS & USES

● If you overheat the mixture you may be able to save it as the split happens by immediately putting a large metal spoon into the custard to reduce the heat, then whisking furiously (without splashing and burning yourself); this may just bring it back together. If it does split completely, though, sieve it, let it cool, introduce a few more egg yolks to the cold liquid and try again.

● If you can't find Greek basil, which is far more perfumed, ordinary will do.

LINK
> Cardamom Sugar, page 226

1 Put the egg yolks, cream, sugar and milk into a heavy-based saucepan. For a stronger cardamom flavour, pop about 8 pods in to infuse. Don't split them, though, or you'll have little black seeds everywhere and the custard will be too thick to sieve.

2 Thicken the mixture by bringing the heat up slowly because the very, very worst thing you can do here is rush. If you boil the liquid, even a tiny bit, you'll have scrambled eggs in no time. The process takes about 15–20 minutes so it's well worth taking it easy. Put the radio on if you're bored. Cogitate life and stir.

3 The mixture will thicken, but it won't set like bought custard – more along the lines of thick double cream. It will set further as it cools. If you want a stronger cardamom flavour then pop about 8 pods in to infuse as the mixture cools.

4 Place the mixture in the fridge until chilled and REMEMBER to pick out any pods once it has cooled. Add the basil and blend until it is incorporated into the ice cream.

5 If using an ice-cream maker, then follow the instructions for churning and freezing. If you're making this by hand, then pour the mixture into a shallow dish (such as a lasagne dish) and whisk it 3–4 times while it's setting – about an hour apart. This prevents ice crystals from forming and you'll get a smooth result. With experience I've learned that it's easy to forget the third and fourth whisking – so I use my timer on the mobile phone.

CARDAMOM CHOCOLATE & VANILLA BISCOTTI

LINKS
> Vanilla Sugar, page 108
> Use Cardamom Sugar (page 226) instead of Vanilla Sugar to intensify the flavour.
> For a festive twist, make Chocolate, Orange & Cardamom Biscotti by using Orange & Clove Sugar (page 245) instead of Vanilla Sugar.

Cardamom & Chocolate Biscotti

Cardamom merges with rich cocoa and soft vanilla. This terrific combination both complements and exaggerates the deeper flavours of coffee like no other biscuit I know. A traditional twice-baked, hard Italian biscuit, these fragrant biscotti can also be served with fruit fool or ice cream. Alternatively, they make an elegant sweet for a supper party. The almond crunch works brilliantly with a plate of baked figs drizzled in honey and a slice of creamy Gorgonzola – an effortless yet classic blend. What I really adore about these biscuits is the fact that it takes so little time to have them made and in the oven. I can also pop half in the freezer, allowing me to cook them fresh at sort notice. Super-fast, super-simple sophistication.

Makes 30
Prep time 25–30 minutes
Cooking time 40–45 minutes
Suitable for freezing
Freeze them after the first bake

300g whole almonds
200g Vanilla Sugar >
350g self-raising flour, plus 1 extra
   spoonful (optional)
50g cocoa powder, sifted
1 level tsp ground cardamom
1 level tsp course sea salt
1 tsp baking powder
6 medium eggs
60g chopped roasted hazelnuts

TIPS & USES

● Use a heavy-duty food mixer such as a Kenwood or KitchenAid. This dough can be very stiff, and a hand-held mixer will not be up to the job!

● Medium eggs vary in size, so if the dough looks a little loose, simply add a heaped tablespoon of flour to stiffen it.

● The final flavour of these biscuits is significantly improved by using freshly ground cardamom.

● A jar of these makes a handsome gift. They store for 1–2 weeks, and improve with age.

1 Preheat the oven 180°C/ gas mark 4. To add a good crunch to the almonds, gently toast them in a heavy-based frying pan on a low heat for about 5 minutes. They should become brittle and more flavoursome. Take care, though, as they burn easily.

2 In a bowl mix the sugar, flour, cocoa powder, cardamom, salt and baking powder together.

3 Using a food mixer, beat the eggs, then slowly add the dry mix to form a loose dough. If the dough looks too loose, add an extra spoonful of flour and mix further. Add the roasted almonds at the end, stirring them in gently – you don't want to break them.

4 Make the dough into 2 'logs' about 25cm long and no more than 10cm wide. Transfer these to a large greased baking tray, leaving a gap between the logs because they expand during baking. Sprinkle evenly with the hazelnuts.

5 Bake for 20–25 minutes. Keep a close eye on them at the end of baking as they can burn easily. Remove from the oven and cool.

6 To avoid the biscuits breaking as you cut through the almonds, use a very sharp knife and cut straight down, pressing the heel of your hand on top of the knife. Don't saw. Cut into 2cm portions, lay each biscuit flat and return the tray to the oven. (You can freeze them at this point.)

7 Bake for 10–12 minutes on each side. Leave on a wire rack for 1–2 hours to dry out completely, then transfer to an airtight container.

Victoria Sponge Cake with Cardamom Rose Cream & Rhubarb

There is something whimsical about this cake. It's soft, feminine and pink, with floral notes and flower petals: the centrepiece for a summer's day tea party. Yet it is quite simple to make, and the combination of flavours is what really sets this one apart. Rhubarb jam adds the sour note that tempers the sweetness, while the cardamom and rose entwine like a tangle of roses on your taste buds. A small slice with a cup of Earl Grey tea in a dainty china cup…how perfectly English can you get?

Serves 8–10
Prep time 30 minutes
Cooking time 20–25 minutes
Suitable for freezing
Before filling or decorating

For the cake
250g butter or margarine
  (suitable for baking)
250g Cardamom Sugar >
250g self-raising flour
4 large eggs

For the filling
400ml double cream
3 drops of rose essence
80g icing sugar (sifted)
200g Rhubarb Jam >

To decorate
150g icing sugar (sifted)
Lemon juice
50g white chocolate curls
Edible rose/geranium petals

1 Preheat the oven to 180°C/gas mark 4. Using a hand mixer or food mixer, cream together the butter or margarine and Cardamom Sugar. Beat well until white and fluffy.

2 Add 3–4 tablespoons of flour to the mixture, then add the eggs. Adding the flour like this prevents the mixture from curdling. If it does, just keep adding flour a little at a time, beating the mixture to ensure it is evenly distributed. Continue mixing and add the rest of the flour.

3 Divide the mixture between two 23cm round cake tins and bake in the oven for 20–25 minutes, until firm to the touch. Cool on a wire rack.

4 Once the cake is fully cooled, make the filling. Whip the cream, rose essence and icing sugar until thick. Spread the jam on the base of one cake and the cream on the other and sandwich together.

5 Mix the icing sugar for the topping with a few drops of lemon juice – use only a drop or two at a time – until you have a viscous mix about the consistency of custard. Pour this over the top of the cake and sprinkle with the white chocolate curls before decorating with edible flowers.

TIPS & USES
● Keep your eggs at room temperature. They get more air in them and you get a lighter batter.

● If you don't have Cardamom Sugar to hand, grind about 10 cardamom pods in a pestle and mortar to release the good seeds inside. Discard the green husk and grind the seeds well into a fine powder.

LINKS
> Rhubarb Jam, page 40
> Cardamom Sugar, page 226

● Oven temperatures vary, so after 20 minutes take a peek. Don't do it before, though, or the blast of cold air can deflate your cake!

● Whenever you grease your tins use a piece of kitchen roll to spread a fine layer of margarine around the edge. To prevent a greasy film from forming on the cake, put a tablespoon of flour in the greased tin and proceed to tap it around the surface.

● The base of this cake is the same as that used in the Vanilla & Rhubarb Cupcakes on page 33 and the same as the Victoria Sandwich Cake. Rather than bake twice, I make double the recipe and pop the base in the freezer – prepped! You can decorate the Victoria Sandwich Cake while it's still frozen and leave it to defrost.

● To get white chocolate curls, run a vegetable peeler along the edge of a white chocolate bar.

Orange & Clove

In the darkest part of December, just the scent of oranges and cloves wafting across the kitchen is a declaration of all that is festive in flavour and spirit. The warmth of the clove and the sweetness of the orange make a winning winter combination.

Cloves alone can prove a strong, overbearing character in the kitchen, but orange lifts and tempers the heavy spice, making this duo unbeatable. This joyful team can't fail to lift your spirits and delight your senses in terms of colour, scent and flavour throughout the Christmas kitchen.

Spiced Orange & Clove Brandy

Cloves are unique in their aromatic warmth and festive connotations. Paired with orange, this is a duo that wraps itself around you, lingering like a delicious kiss in your mouth. In this brandy, it continues its theme throughout this chapter, adding depth and festive spirit (no pun intended) across many recipes. To me, it tastes like you're sitting by a crackling fire on Christmas Eve as the carol singers arrive.

Makes almost a full 1-litre bottle
Prep time 3 minutes

700ml brandy
3 cloves
2 cinnamon sticks
Zest of 1 large orange
250g caster sugar

1 Put all the ingredients into a sterilized glass bottle and make sure the lid is closed tightly.

2 To mix the sugar and brandy, shake the bottle several times a day during the course of a week. The sugar will dissolve, leaving you with a beautiful amber liqueur that has a heavenly viscosity about it.

> **LINK**
> > Brandy Butter, page 246

Festive Cocktail

To be fair, it's being perhaps a little generous to call this a cocktail. It's more like a long drink. But whatever you call it, it's easy to make, and ideal to sling together in seconds, leaving you free to chat with friends if they pop in. It's warm, spiced and goes rather well with a mince pie or two!

Per cocktail
50ml Spiced Orange & Clove Brandy **>** (above)
About 175ml ginger beer

1 Pour the brandy into a tall ice-filled glass and top it up with the ginger beer.

> **LINKS**
> > Chicken Liver Parfait, page 249
> > Roast Pork Belly with Orange & Cloves, page 250
> > Cranberry & Brandy Mincemeat, page 253
> > Christmas Puddings, page 260
> > My Grandmother's Christmas Cake, page 264

Orange & Clove Sugar

This sugar delivers a wallop of Christmas in a jar. The deep flavour of cloves is lifted by the sweet orange in an intense combination. You can add this to almost any recipe to infuse festivity: custard, ice cream, a hot chocolate or any cake recipes, including chocolate cake. Or you can simply open the jar and take a deep breath every now and again – the aroma is just heavenly!

Makes 1 large (1.2kg) jar
Prep time 10 minutes
Cooking time 2 hours

Zest and peel of 6 oranges
18 cloves
1.2kg caster sugar

1 Preheat the oven to 140°C/gas mark 1.

2 Using a vegetable peeler, peel the oranges and ensure there is very little pith attached to the zest.

3 Place the peel on a tray and dry it gently in the oven for about 1½–2 hours.

4 Once the peel is dry, place half the cloves and half the orange zest in a blender with 600g of sugar. Give it a good blast until they are well-blended. Mix in the rest of the sugar, cloves and orange and transfer to an airtight jar.

TIP
● I'd say use within 3 months – but generally it's gone in a week!

LINKS
> This sugar links to most recipes in this chapter.
> Use instead of regular sugar in Lemon Cake (page 105) and Caraway Biscotti (page 199).
> Use instead of Vanilla Sugar in Rice Pudding (page 121), Vanilla Custard (page 118), Crème Brûlée (page 122), and Vanilla Blondies (page 125).

Brandy Butter

If time is short and you want to impress, make your own brandy butter. I make mine two different ways, depending on which sugar I have in the cupboard. The sweetest is made with icing sugar. It's the same as the shop-bought one, but with your own level of brandy added. The second is made with soft brown sugar and has a deeper, more toffeed flavour. What's most important is that you use it at the last minute (i.e. straight from the fridge), as the contrast between the cold butter and the hot mince pies makes it all the more delicious.

Makes 400g: enough for about 25 mince pies
Prep time 5 minutes

200g butter
200g soft brown sugar OR icing sugar
8 tbsp Spiced Orange & Clove Brandy >

> ### LINKS
> > Spiced Orange & Clove Brandy:
>   page 242
> > Brandy Butter, page 254
> > Eccles Cakes, page 263

1 In a blender or with an electric hand mixer, blend the butter and sugar together until the mixture is soft and light.

2 Add the brandy just 1 tablespoon at a time and keep mixing.

3 Transfer to an airtight container and keep in the fridge.

TIP
● Check the use-by date on the butter; your brandy butter will keep until then.

LINKS
> A dollop of Rhubarb Jam (page 40) goes down
  a treat with this pâté, as does a sweet chutney
  or jam. I serve it with Spiced Tomato Jam
  (page 128) or Plum Chutney (page 163).
> Try Plum Brandy (page 156) instead of Spiced
  Orange & Clove Brandy, using pink peppercorns
  instead of the orange and cloves as garnish.
> Spiced Orange & Clove Brandy, page 242

Chicken Liver Parfait

This is utterly delicious! It didn't cross my mind for years that it's such a cinch to make, but having said that, it wasn't the easiest recipe to develop in order to get the luxurious, light, smooth finish. In the end it was Gary Jones, executive head chef at Michelin two-star restaurant Le Manoir, in Oxford, who gave me the method below. (Thank you!) It's not the quickest dish (it takes an hour), but you do end up with one to eat now and one for the freezer. It makes a great prepped starter for Christmas lunch, and is a welcome food gift when you're expected to turn up at a party bearing goodies. Note: you'll need a food processor for this one.

Makes 2; each terrine serves 8–10 as a starter
Prep time 30 minutes
Cooking time 1 hour
Suitable for freezing

800g prepared frozen chicken
   livers, defrosted
6 eggs, at room temperature
500g salted butter, melted
120ml Orange & Clove Brandy >
1 large pinch of sea salt
Zest of 1 orange, plus extra to garnish
1 level tsp caster sugar
6 bay leaves
160g ghee

TIPS & USES

● Use only frozen chicken livers: this reduces the amount of *Campylobacter* that might be present, which can lead to food poisoning. Using frozen livers has no effect on the finished product.

● Make one day ahead of needing to use.

● This parfait keeps for three days in the fridge, or you can freeze it. It's slightly more crumbly if frozen (but only slightly).

● If you don't have Orange & Clove Brandy, use ordinary brandy – it's still delicious.

1 Preheat the oven to 140°/gas mark 1.

2 Put the chicken livers and eggs into a food processor and blend until they are liquidised. Strain through a large sieve into a jug.

3 Add the melted butter, brandy, salt, zest and sugar. Mix well.

4 Divide the mixture between two 1kg loaf-tin-shaped containers. Leave enough room for the ghee! I use a silicone mould, but you can line the tins or dishes with cling film. Cover both dishes with foil to stop water getting in.

5 Place the containers into a deep baking dish to act as a bain-marie. Fill the bain-marie with very hot water two-thirds the way up the tins and pop the lot into the oven. Cook for 1 hour. To test if the parfait is done, use a temperature probe inserted into the middle; the temperature should be above 73°C. The parfait should have a light wobble (but not too much).

6 Remove from the oven and cool to room temperature before putting 3 bay leaves on the top of each 'loaf', pouring the melted ghee on top and then scattering the extra orange zest on top of that. Place in the fridge to set overnight.

7 To serve, cut it into slices by dipping a sharp knife into very hot water; this gives a clean finish. Serve with toast and a dollop of Rhubarb or Plum Jam.

Roast Pork Belly with Orange & Cloves

As Christmas approaches, my purse and my spare time inevitably seem to shrink in unison – which is one reason I adore this recipe. This ultra-simple dish is now a favourite in many restaurants, especially as these cheaper cuts of meat have become so fashionable. It has a crisp, crunchy crackling with melt-in-the-mouth sweet meat alongside the aromatic, festive orange and cloves. What's more, I challenge anyone to take more than ten minutes to get it into the oven!

Serves 6
Prep time 10 minutes
Cooking time 6 hours

6 garlic cloves, whole and unpeeled
Peel of 1 orange, made using a vegetable
 peeler to get large strips
15 whole cloves
1 cinnamon stick
1.5kg pork belly, scored
 (ask your butcher to do this)
2 tbsp sea salt
35ml Spiced Orange & Clove Brandy **>**
100ml orange juice
1 tsp sugar

1 Preheat your oven to its full whack: at least 220°C/gas mark 7.

2 In a roasting tin, put the garlic cloves, orange peel, 8 cloves and the cinnamon stick on the bottom, underneath where the pork will be.

3 Rub the underside of the pork belly with half the salt and rub the other half into the skin.

4 Press the remaining 7 cloves into the skin, place the pork in the roasting tin and pop it into the oven. Drop the heat to 150°C/gas mark 2 and cook for 5–6 hours, until tender.

5 Remove from the heat, take the meat out of the pan, and set it to one side to rest. Strain the juices into a pan, add the brandy and heat up until boiling. Slowly add the orange juice and sugar. Boil this for 2–3 minutes to reduce the liquid and concentrate the taste of the sauce.

6 Slice the pork, drizzle it with the sauce and serve with pan-fried potatoes and rosemary.

> **LINK**
> **>** Spiced Orange & Clove Brandy, page 242

Instant Cranberry & Brandy Mincemeat

If there is one time of year to be a domestic goddess, it really has to be Christmas. But with all the extra demands on your time there are never enough hours in the day, and the idea of making mincemeat used to send me a little bit closer to a festive breakdown. That is, until I came across a recipe for fresh mincemeat by food writer Nigella Lawson. This isn't her recipe, but it was certainly inspired by her idea. I keep a pot in the fridge as an emergency present as it is generally well-received by anyone. It's simple to make, packed full of Christmas flavour and guaranteed to make you feel like a domestic goddess. Happiness in a jar!

Makes 2 x 440g jars
Prep time 15 minutes
Cooking time 15 minutes

200g soft brown sugar
170ml Spiced Orange & Clove Brandy **>**
300g fresh cranberries
170g dried cherries or blueberries
  (or a mixture)
200g mixed currants and raisins
30g peeled, very finely grated
  fresh ginger
2 tsp mixed spice
Juice and zest of 2 medium oranges
1 vanilla pod, cut into 4 pieces

1 Put the sugar and brandy into a large pan and warm gently. Add the fresh cranberries and cook gently for about 3 minutes. Stir well.

2 Tip in the dried fruit, ginger, mixed spice, orange juice and zest and vanilla, and stir well. Cover and simmer very gently for about 15 minutes, stirring and checking occasionally.

3 Spoon into clean jars and store in the fridge. This keeps happily for up to 2 weeks.

> ### LINKS
> **>** Spiced Orange & Clove Brandy, page 242
> **>** Baked Apples, page 254
> **>** Mince Pies, page 259

Baked Apples

On a weekday evening when you don't have enough energy to consider making a pudding, this one will fit the bill. It is so simple and quick that even the weariest person can hollow out an apple, open a jar and fill the resulting hole to produce a warm, comforting, restorative spiced dessert. If you have any left over, they're delicious as a cold breakfast with a sprinkle of granola and a dollop of yogurt.

Serves 6
Prep time 10 minutes
Cooking time 25 minutes

6 medium baking apples
  (about 250g each)
440g Instant Cranberry & Brandy
  Mincemeat **>**
60g Brandy Butter **>**

1 Preheat the oven to 150°C/gas mark 2.

2 Use an apple corer to remove the entire core and a small amount of the surrounding flesh of each apple. Fill the hole with three tablespoons of mincemeat. Pop a teaspoon of Brandy Butter on top and bake in an ovenproof dish for 20–25 minutes.

3 Serve with more Brandy Butter or make custard using Orange & Clove Sugar.

LINKS
> Orange & Clove Sugar, page 245
> Brandy Butter, page 246
> Instant Cranberry & Brandy
  Mincemeat, page 253

Mince Pies

Deep-filled, fruity, almond-topped mince pies. If there is one thing Christmas means to me, it's the chance to eat mince pies – lots of them. It's not as if we eat them at any other time of year, so their rare appearance warrants making your own, especially as I haven't yet bitten into a shop-bought one and not instantly regretted it! These mince pies are probably the nicest in the world, ever. Just be warned that carol singers may do several encores for more of them!

Makes 12
Prep time 30 minutes
Cooking time 30 minutes
Suitable for freezing

For the pastry
250g plain flour
   (00 is good but not essential)
Pinch of salt
50g icing sugar
125g butter
2 egg yolks, beaten
30ml ice-cold water

For the filling
440g Instant Cranberry & Brandy
   Mincemeat **>**
Frangipane, made with Orange &
   Clove Sugar **>**
Flaked almonds, to scatter

LINKS
> Frangipane, page 48
> I highly recommend a gentle
   warming in the oven before eating
   with Brandy Butter (page 246).
> Instant Cranberry & Brandy
   Mincemeat, page 253.

1 Preheat the oven to 175°C/gas mark 3.

2 Sift the flour, salt and icing sugar into a mixing bowl. Cut the butter into cubes in the flour, then rub between the fingertips until the mixture resembles fine breadcrumbs. Don't overdo this. Keep your fingers deliberately light; it is essential to keep the mixture as cold as possible for the best texture.

3 Add the egg yolks and a little of the water and mix into a firm dough with a metal spoon. Use your judgment with the water: add a few drops at a time and mix. Too much can make the pastry too wet.

4 Add the water until the dough comes together. Once it does, quickly use your hands to form a ball, wrap it in cling film, and allow it to rest in the refrigerator for 30 minutes before using.

5 Roll out onto a floured board to about 30cm x 35cm or so. Using a large (8–10cm) biscuit cutter, cut 12 circles and place them gently into a lightly greased muffin tin.

6 Spoon a tablespoon of mincemeat into each pastry circle. Gently press the mincemeat flat with the back of the spoon.

7 Spoon a tablespoon of frangipane over each spoonful of mincemeat, gently easing the mixture to the edge of the pastry. Scatter with flaked almonds and pop in the oven for 25–30 minutes.

8 Remove from the oven and leave for 5 minutes to set a little. Place each pie carefully onto a wire rack; when completely cool, they need to go into an airtight tin. Use within a week.

Christmas Puddings

Really, if there were one thing I would never miss out on, it's making the Christmas pudding. You get one chance a year to make it, and it's so straightforward – and I love making it in advance. This recipe makes two, because if you're going to make one then it's just as easy to make a second as a standby or gift. The mixture here is an 80-year-old recipe from my grandmother, modernised with the phenomenal Heston Blumenthal-style candied orange in the centre. Bearing this in mind, the oranges take a couple of days to candy in a pan of sugar syrup – so be sure to prep your oranges in advance!

Makes 2 puddings; each serves 8
Prep time 2 days and 1 hour
Cooking time 6 hours
Suitable for freezing? Yes, but they will keep for 12 months if sealed.

You will need 2 x 20cm-diameter pudding basins

For the candied oranges
2 navel oranges
1kg sugar
1 cinnamon stick
5 cloves
5 cardamom pods
1 litre water

For the puddings
900g mixed dried fruit
150g blanched almonds, chopped
200g glacé cherries
225g plain flour
200g breadcrumbs
200g Orange & Clove Sugar >
Pinch of salt
2 level tsp mixed spice
400g chopped suet
Zest of 1 lemon
Zest of 1 orange
8 eggs, beaten
150ml Plum Brandy >
   or Spiced Orange & Clove Brandy >
150ml milk
Butter, for greasing

1 To candy the oranges: pierce them half a dozen times all over with a skewer then boil them in water for 30 minutes to soften. Remove them from the water and set them to one side. Discard the water and pop all the other ingredients for the candied oranges into the pan. Bring to the boil.

2 Return the oranges to the pan and cook over a slow heat for 2 hours. Cover for some of the time so that the fruit cooks evenly. Remove from the syrup and leave overnight on a rack, then return to the syrup the following day to boil for about 10 minutes. Allow to cool and then remove them from the syrup (reserve this to make marmalade; see tip) and allow them to dry again; the oranges are now ready!

3 Now make the pudding: mix together all the dry ingredients, the suet and the orange and lemon zest.

4 Stir in the eggs, brandy and milk and mix well.

5 Lightly grease the pudding basins. Spoon a good dollop of mixture into each and put an orange in the centre. Gently add the rest of the mixture so that the orange is covered. Pat it down. Pop on a circle of baking parchment, then put foil over the top of each.

6 Tie securely with string. By tying the string longer, you'll create a string 'handle' from one side of the basin to the other, making it easier to pick the basin out of the pan when it is done.

7 Put the bowls into a good-size steamer (or large pan; see tip on page 261) with boiling water and cover. This will need to boil for about 6 hours. Check regularly to ensure that the water does not boil dry.

8 Cool. Change the baking parchment and foil covers for fresh ones and tie up as before. Store in a cool cupboard until Christmas Day.

9 To serve: steam for 2 hours and serve with Brandy Butter, rum sauce, cream or homemade custard.

TIPS & USES

● If you don't have a steamer, put the pudding basins in a large pan on inverted saucers or on an old tea towel on the base, just so the the basins aren't touching the base of the pan directly. Pour boiling water about a third of the way up the sides of the pudding basins, cover and steam.

● If you boil the leftover syrup from the oranges it makes a super 'no bits' sort of marmalade. Once the oranges are removed, bring to the boil for about 5 minutes. To check setting point, simply drop some on a cold saucer, wait a few minutes and if it wrinkles as you run your finger though it then it will set. Pour into a sterilized jar; you'll get about 450g (give or take, according to how much has evaporated).

LINKS

> Serve with Custard on page 118 made with Orange & Clove Sugar instead of Vanilla Sugar.
> Plum Brandy, page 156
> Spiced Orange & Clove Brandy, page 242
> Orange & Clove Sugar, page 245
> Brandy Butter, page 246

Eccles Cakes

After all the Christmas festivities I often end up with a leftover pot of brandy butter. It's not that I didn't mean to eat it, but inevitably, as January comes, I feel it has had its day. This recipe is a great way to use up the leftover butter, infusing the brandy, orange and cloves into a frugal yet delicious batch of Eccles cakes. Oliver Cromwell banned the original Eccles cakes because they were considered too rich and sumptuous. But, frugal or not, somehow I don't think he would approve of these; they're still seriously hedonistic!

Makes 9
Prep time 20 minutes
Cooking time 20 minutes
Suitable for freezing

1 x 375g pack sweet shortcrust pastry
  (or sweet pastry >)
75g Brandy Butter > softened
200g currants
1 beaten egg, to glaze
3 tbsp Orange & Clove Sugar >,
  for sprinkling

1 Preheat the oven to 180°C/gas mark 4.

2 Roll out the shortcrust pastry to about 6–7 mm thick. Using a 10cm pastry cutter, cut 9 circles (cut the first 7, then bring the pastry together again and re-roll to achieve 9). Use plenty of flour to dust with underneath and don't over-handle the pastry: this makes it tough.

3 Mix the butter and currants well together in a bowl.

4 Put a pastry circle in your left hand (I'm assuming you're right-handed here!) and put a large tablespoon – approximately 30g – of the butter-currant filling into the centre. Bring your fingers together gently around the circle, and as the pastry edges touch, simply pinch them together, using your right hand to seal the parcel.

5 Place pinched-side down a very lightly greased baking sheet. Gently squash it down using the palm of your hand to make it into a patty shape.

6 Once all the cakes are made, brush them all over with the egg for a glaze and dust liberally with the sugar. Cut 3 small slits on the top and bake for 18–20 minutes, or until they are golden brown. Place on a wire rack and allow to cool before transferring to an airtight container.

LINKS
> Cardamom Sugar, page 226
> Orange & Clove Sugar, page 245
> Brandy Butter, page 246
> Pastry, 259

TIP
● If you don't have any flavoured sugar to hand, add the zest of an orange into the currants to infuse more orange flavour into the cakes.

My Grandmother's Christmas Cake

This is my grandmother's cake. She made wedding, christening and Christmas cakes for a living, and this recipe is over 80 years old. I was given the original recipe by my mother while I was researching this book. I'm told that in the 1950s and '60s, Grandmother's cakes were so amazing that people travelled from miles around to order one. I'm also told that cake-making was quite a sociable occasion. Helen at Gardener's Bakery in Northampton decorated the beautiful cake in these pictures, and I know if my grandmother could see this now, she'd be so proud of me she'd have to tell everyone (and anyone) all about it!

Makes 16 slices
Prep time 25–30 minutes
Cooking time 4–5 hours

250g self-raising flour
A pinch salt
½ tsp bicarbonate of soda
½ tsp ground cloves
½ tsp cinnamon
½ tsp mixed spice
200g butter
Zest of 1 lemon
200g sugar
2 heaped tbsp treacle
2 tsp vanilla essence
6 eggs, beaten
450g sultanas
220g raisins
300g currants
20 glacé cherries
100g chopped nuts
Spiced Orange & Clove Brandy **>**
  to feed the cake

TIP
● To make gifts, quarter this cake to create 4 small cakes serving 4 slices each.

LINKS
> Use Plum Brandy (page 156) instead of Spiced Orange & Clove Brandy.
> Spiced Orange & Clove Brandy, page 242

1 Preheat the oven to 150°C/gas mark 2

2 Sieve the flour, salt, bicarbonate of soda and spices into a bowl.

3 Cream the butter, lemon zest and sugar in a large mixing bowl. Mix in the treacle, and vanilla essence until light and fluffy.

4 Mix in the eggs a little at a time. To stop the batter from curdling add a tablespoon of the flour. Fold in the remaining flour. Mix well, then fold in the dried fruit, glacé cherries and chopped nuts.

5 Grease a 20cm round or 18cm square cake tin and line the bottom and sides with baking parchment. Turn the mixture into the tin and make a slight hollow in the centre to keep the cake flat on top. You don't want to decorate a domed cake!

6 Bake for 1 hour, then turn the oven down to 140°C/gas mark 1 for about 3½–4 hours. Push a skewer into the centre to test for doneness. If it doesn't come out clean, return the cake to the oven for up to another hour. Test every 20 minutes or so until the skewer comes out clean. Remove from the oven. Leave to cool in the tin for 20 minutes.

7 Turn out onto a wire rack. Once the cake is completely cool, poke a few holes in it with a skewer and pour over 3–4 tbsp of Spiced Orange & Clove Brandy. Let the brandy soak right into the cake. Keep the cake wrapped in foil and in an airtight tin or plastic container, with the holes-side up. Spoon over 2–3 tablespoons every week until you decorate the cake.

Christmas Cake.

Bake at Slow oven. 300 F

at. Mark 1 for 1 hr. then red.

Heat to 275 F or Mark ½

continue to Bake for ...

10 oz. Self Raising Flour

1 lb. Sultanas.

... Raisins.

... currants.

... mixed Cherries.

... ...

Index

Acknowledgements

Thank you

For words of encouragement and seriously good advice
Heather Holden Brown, for introducing me to How To Books and her words of guidance. Jason Atherton, for his words of encouragement and praise. Louise Mackeness, for her constant advice on styling the photography. Tim Hayward, for his time and advice on the publishing industry. Heidi Wallace, for her words of support. Sophie Grigson, for her time and effort in guiding the clarity of *Prepped!* Nigel Slater, for his kind words and inspiration. Gary Jones, of Le Manoir, for help with the Chicken Liver Parfait recipe. Fleur Seals, for pushing me to follow the idea. Chantal Coady of Rococo Chocolates, for her constant support throughout. Laura Tenison, for getting the concept instantly and saying so. To BBC Radio Northampton, John Griff and Mark Whall, for constantly giving me the opportunity to broadcast my recipes, and David Summers of *Northampton Chronicle and Echo*. To Bobby's Restaurant, Leicester, for teaching me to make barfi properly. To Waterstone's in Midsummer Place, Milton Keynes, for allowing me to research in the store.

For lending me their kitchens and gardens to do the photography
Mick and Anne Andreaol, Cathinka Borkran, Sir Peter and Judy Ellwood, Emma Hodgeson, Flora Hulme, Lucy Lewis, Melissa Lewis (and Issy Lewis for being the prop!), Margaret Lever, Gill Parton, and Susie Pasley-Tyler of Coton Manor Gardens.

For lending me props for the photography
Cabbages and Roses; Carnival Taylor, Northampton; Henrietta Flynn from www.CookingGorgeous.com; De Gouray wallpaper; KitchenAid; The Kitchen Range Cookshop, Market Harborough, www.kitchenrangecookshop.com; The Natural Floor Company, Northampton; Patteson's Glass, www.jarsandbottles.co.uk; Porsche Knives, for the best knives there are; Stephanie from Rococo Antiques in Weedon; The Spon, www.thesponco.com; Troops and Son, Brixworth; Xing Xing, www.xingxingltd.com.

For supplying ingredients
For the hugely generous Lulu Sturdy of Ndali Vanilla, for supplying all fairtrade organic vanilla. www.ndali.net. Chantal Coady of Rococo Chocolates, for kindness and support in supplying all fairtrade organic chocolate for *Prepped!*

For testing my recipes at home
Jessica Appleford, Cathinka Borkan, Robyn Brook, Audrey Dean, Alison Macpherson, Tara McAndrew, Fleur Seals, Catherine Sharman, Ella Swannell and Sarah-Jane van der Westhuizen.

For testing my recipes and blogging about them
Shirin Amchin – www.diaryofamessykitchen.blogspot.com
Ren Behan – www.renbehan.com
Helen Best-Shaw – www.fussfreeflavours.com
Ross Boyce – www.itinerantappetite.blogspot.com
Jennie Brotherston – www.allthethingsieat.blogspot.com
Katie Bryson – www.feedingboys.wordpress.com
Joanna Cary – www.anenglishkitchen.com
Christine Chan – www.thebountifulplate.wordpress.com
Ruth Clemens – www.thepinkwhisk.co.uk
Audrey Deane – www.audreydeane.posterous.com
Jo Dyson – www.joskitchen.wordpress.com
Susan M Easton – www.notjustanyoldbaking.blogspot.com
Julie Elliott – www.angelinacupcakes.blogspot.com

Danielle Ellis – www.edinburghfoody.com
Jules Gilbert – www.thebutcherthebaker.wordpress.com
Lorne Gray – www.grazeandguzzle.com
Lea Harris – www.OfftheEatenTrack.wordpress.com
Alethea Hill – www.mom-on-a-wire.blogspot.com
Lynne Hill – www.bakelady.wordpress.com
Rebecca Hodgson – www.rebeccabakescakes.blogspot.com
Jeane Horak Druiff – www.cooksister.com
Rebecca Hutchinson – www.iwannabeadomesticgoddess.com
Amy Lane – www.amylane.wordpress.com
Jayne Lynch – www.jaynerly.wordpress.com
Mangocheeks – www.allotment2kitchen.blogspot.com
Claire Melvin – www.claireshandmadecakes.com
Anita Menon – www.sliceofmylyfe.wordpress.com
Jayne Miller – www.veggieinspain.com
Helen Parkins – www.aforkfulofspaghetti.blogspot.com
Helen Redfern – www.helenredfern.com
Tracey Reilly – www.nippy-sweetie.blogspot.com
Andrea Robson – www.madewithpink.com
Ross Shand – www.chargingchimp.posterous.com
Sarah Trivuncic – www.maisoncupcake.com
Caroline von Schmalensee – www.edinburghfoody.com
Rachel Wald – www.midthirtieslife.com
Becky Wiggins – www.englishmum.com

For emergency childcare!
Cathinka Borkan, Robyn Brook, Margaret Lever, and Flora Hulme (aka my mum!).

For proofreading *Prepped!*
Cathinka Borkan, Lea Harris, Alethea Hill and Fleur Seals.

Calligraphy for all the labels throughout *Prepped!* www.joydaniels.co.uk

Photography
To Brian Dunstone: my thanks seem little indeed for the hours and hours you have spent working with me. Tony Hardacre: thank you – it's stunning. For taking shots for me: Sarah Browne and Louise Smith.

And...
Katie Read of Orange Square, for her tireless and successful efforts on behalf of a first-time author.

To Nikki Read and Giles Lewis of How To Books and their team, for spotting the potential and being supportive, professional, passionate and principled.

To Jamie Ambrose, for keeping my voice, catching the mistakes and fine-tuning the words.

To Ian Hughes, for translating the vision into this beautiful design – www.mousematdesign.com.

Special thanks to my family for their constant love and support: my husband, Alastair; my children: Libiana, William and Isobel; and especially my mum and dad. Extra gratitude to my sister-in-law, Kellie, and my sister, Fleur, for emotional propping, and my friend Cathinka, for her constant friendship and honesty.